STUDY GUIDE

to accompany

ELECTRONICS FUNDAMENTALS: CIRCUITS, DEVICES AND APPLICATIONS

by THOMAS L. FLOYD

Prepared by

Wally McIntyre

DeVry Institute of Technology, Chicago

Merrill Publishing Company
A Bell & Howell Information Company
Columbus Toronto London Melbourne

Cover Photo: Merrill Publishing/Larry Hamill

Published by Merrill Publishing Company
A Bell & Howell Information Company
Columbus, Ohio 43216

Administrative Editor: Stephen Helba
Production Coordinator: JoEllen Gohr
Art Coordinator: Patrick Welch
Cover Designer: Cathy Watterson

International Standard Book Number: 0-675-20676-6

Printed in the United States of America

4 5 6 7 8 9 -- 92 91 90

CONTENTS

PREFACE

TO THE STUDENT:

This study guide can be a valuable learning aid as you explore the fascinating world of electronics. After you read each chapter of the text, you can reinforce your mastery of the subjects by reading the chapter summary in this study guide. Then the chapter quizzes will help define areas where your understanding of the material may be weak. Take the quizzes; if you miss some questions, then reread the related concepts in the text or in this study guide. Once you have gained full mastery of each chapter, you can progress to the next one. May your new career in electronics be interesting and rewarding.

TO THE INSTRUCTOR:

This study guide is arranged with many multiple-choice questions at the end of each chapter. These sheets may be torn out and assigned as homework or classroom assignments, or they may be used as quizzes. Many of my students report that the study guide concept is of benefit to them if the instructor uses the material as listed above. I welcome your feedback.

ACKNOWLEDGMENTS

My thanks to Dick Bridgeman (DeVry - Lombard) and Tom Floyd for their valuable suggestions toward improving this study guide. Also, I appreciate the efforts of the entire Production team at Merrill, including Tanya Tiberi, Ann Mirels, Bruce Johnson, JoEllen Gohr, Tim McEwen, and Steve Helba.

REVIEW OF KEY POINTS IN CHAPTER 1

INTRODUCTION

HISTORY

- The word **electricity** was used by Sir Thomas Browne (1605-82).
- Benjamin Franklin theorized that electricity was a fluid.
- Charles Coulomb proposed the laws of charge in 1785.
- Volt, a unit of potential energy, was named after Alessandro Volta (1745-1827).
- Electromagnetism was discovered in 1820 by Hans Oersted.
- The ampere, a unit of current, was named after André Ampère. He laid the fundamental laws that are basic to electricity.
- Ohm's law, named after Georg Simon Ohm in 1826, forms the basis for relationships among voltage, resistance, and current.
- The electronic age started in 1909, when Robert Millikan measured the charge on an electron.
- The year 1904 saw the invention of the first vacuum tube by John Fleming.
- The first practical amplifier device, an audion, was built in 1907 by Lee de Forest.
- Television picture tubes got their start in the 1920s by Vladimir Zworykin's invention of the kinescope.
- Digital computers got started in 1946 at the University of Pennsylvania.
- The transistor was discovered in 1948 at Bell Labs.
- Integrated circuits came into being in the early 1960s.

CAREERS IN ELECTRONICS

- The service shop technician works in an electronic repair facility. He or she could repair any type of electronic equipment.
- The manufacturing technician works in a plant, either testing equipment or maintaining testing equipment.
- The laboratory technician works closely with engineers, breadboarding circuits and making tests for the engineer.
- The field service technician services and repairs electronic equipment at the customer's location.
- The technical writer prepares manuals for the use and service of electronic equipment.
- The technical salesperson is responsible for sales of high-technology products.

CIRCUIT COMPONENTS

- **Resistors** resist the flow of electric current in a circuit.
- **Capacitors** store electric charge.
- **Inductors** are used to store energy in an electromagnetic field.
- **Transformers** are used to couple ac voltages between circuits and to increase or decrease ac voltages.
- **Semiconductor devices** are diodes, transistors, and integrated circuits.

ELECTRICAL UNITS

- Engineers and scientists must use common terms when communicating with each other. Each electric quantity must have a unique reference name. Some examples are volts for voltage, amperes for current, ohms for resistance, farads for capacitance, and henrys for inductance. There are many more.

SCIENTIFIC NOTATION AND METRIC PREFIXES

- Scientific notation and metric prefixes are convenient ways of expressing both very large and very small numbers. For example, 0.000006 in scientific notation is 6×10^{-6}. Standard metric prefixes are used to make unit expressions even shorter; that is, $6 \times 10^{-6} = 6\mu$.

- Scientific notation and metric prefixes are adaptable to the modern calculator.

TECHNICIAN TIPS

- Upon completion of your electronic education, you will be seeking a good-paying, interesting job. Your future employer will be looking at your technical qualifications and sometimes of even more importance--your attitude. Are you enthusiastic, outgoing, pleasant? Will you fit into the working place? Your attitude and outlook on life will be of great influence to the selection of you as a new employee.

- Learning the shortcuts to electronic terminology will speed you on your career. This field is filled with these abbreviations. Some of these are F for farad, E or V for voltage, I for current, f for frequency, Hz for cycles per second. The list is long, so be prepared for the new language of electronics.

- The term **powers of ten** describes a mathematical notation that you will use to make your understanding of electronic measurements and terms much easier. It is a shortcut to using the large and small numbers used in electronics. Use the powers of ten to communicate with your calculator. This will be indispensable to you as you study the text.

- Metric prefixes will help you to speak and write the language of electronics. As an example, 25,000,000 ohms can be expressed as 25 Megohms. As another example, 0.000000000035 farad can be expressed as 35×10^{-12} or even simpler 35 pf since the prefix "p" means 10^{-12}. See how each simplification gets the terms shorter and easier to use.

CHAPTER 1 QUIZ

Student Name____

1. Georg Simon Ohm developed Ohm's law in about 1820.
   a. true
   b. false

2. Many careers exist for the electronic technician.
   a. true
   b. false

3. The unit of current is the ampere.
   a. true
   b. false

4. 15,000 V can be expressed in powers of ten as 15×10^3.
   a. true
   b. false

5. 0.0015 A can be expressed in metric units as 1.5 mA.
   a. true
   b. false

6. Some typical careers for electronic technicians are
   a. as technical writers
   b. as technical salespersons
   c. as manufacturing technicians
   d. as service shop technicians
   e. all of the above

7. A circuit component that resists the flow of current in a circuit is known as
   a. a capacitor
   b. an inductor
   c. a resistor
   d. a transformer

8. A circuit component that stores electric charge is
   a. a transformer
   b. a capacitor
   c. a resistor
   d. an inductor
   e. a semiconductor

9. Some semiconductor devices are
   a. transformers, transistors, and integrated circuits.
   b. diodes, transistors, and resistors.
   c. integrated circuits, inductors, and capacitors.
   d. integrated circuits, capacitors, and diodes.
   e. diodes, transistors, and integrated circuits.

10. The electrical symbol for capacitance is
   a. I
   b. V
   c. C
   d. Q
   e. E

11. The symbol A is an abbreviation for
   a. farad
   b. volt
   c. hertz
   d. henry
   e. ampere

12. A device that stores energy electromagnetically is
   a. a capacitor
   b. an inductor
   c. a transistor
   d. a diode

13. The symbol and unit for time is
   a. t, I
   b. C, f
   c. t, s
   d. Z, W

14. The value 4.7×10^3 Ω can be expressed as
   a. 0.00047 Ω
   b. 4.7 kΩ
   c. 4.7 Ω
   d. 4.7 MΩ

15. You have just calculated an answer for a problem. Your calculator reads 3.5-06. The correct metric value is
   a. 35 milli-
   b. 35 micro-
   c. 3.5 mega-
   d. 3.5 micro-
   e. 3.5 pico-

16. You are trying to enter 45,600 Ω into your calculator. A correct entry might be
    a. 4.56 03
    b. 4.56-03
    c. 456 01
    d. 4.56 04
    e. 45.6 05

17. Your calculator gives you an answer on its display of 1.2 05. A correct metric value of resistance for this answer is
    a. 12 kΩ
    b. 0.12 MΩ
    c. 12,000 Ω
    d. 1200 Ω

18. The correct expression for 7.84×10^{-8} F is
    a. 784 pF
    b. 0.0784 μF
    c. 7.84 μF
    d. 7840 μF

19. Express these calculator displays in correct metric values: 4.7-06, 1.5 04, 9.5-03

a.	47 milli-	15000	9.5 milli-
b.	470	1500	0.095 micro-
c.	4.7 micro-	15 kilo-	9.5 milli-
d.	470 milli-	15 kilo-	9.5 milli-

20. Express 5.6×10^{-2} in milli-, basic units, and micro-.

a.	5.6	0.056	56000
b.	56	0.056	56000
c.	560	5.6	5600
d.	5600	56	560

REVIEW OF KEY POINTS IN CHAPTER 2

THE BASIC ELECTRICAL QUANTITIES

ELECTRONS

- **Free electrons**, found in some atoms, are capable of moving easily from one atom to another.
- **Conductors** are materials that have large numbers of free electrons available to move.
- **Semiconductors** are materials that have fewer free electrons. Due to their special nature, devices like diodes and transistors use this material.
- **Insulators** are materials that have few free electrons so that they do not conduct current easily.

ELECTRICAL CHARGE

- **Electrons** are negatively charged particles.
- Particles with the same charge repel each other.
- Particles with different charges attract each other.
- The **coulomb** is a unit of charge that contains 6.25×10^{18} electrons.
- The symbol for charge is Q.

VOLTAGE

- **Voltage** is the force that exists between charged particles.
- The unit of voltage is the **volt** and the symbol is either V or E.
- Some other names for voltage are electromotive force (emf) and potential difference.
- A battery is a source of voltage. It uses a chemical action to produce quantities of electrons.

- The electronic power supply uses commercial electric utility power to supply voltage.
- The solar cell operates as a direct conversion unit between sunlight and voltage.
- A generator takes mechanical energy, usually rotating, and produces a voltage.

CURRENT

- **Current** is the movement of free electrons. It comes about when a voltage is applied to a closed circuit.
- Electron current flows or moves from negative toward the positive.
- The electrical symbol for current is I.
- The basic unit of current is the **ampere**. It is defined as the charge Q (number of coulombs) that moves past any point in one second of time.

$$I = Q/t$$

RESISTANCE

- **Resistance** is the opposition to the movement of current.
- The electrical symbol for resistance is R.
- The basic unit is the **ohm**.
- **Resistors** are components that are designed to have a resistance or opposition of various amounts.
- **Fixed resistors** are devices that have a fixed amount of resistance, such as 47 ohms or 1.2 Megohms.
- The **resistor color code** is a system used to mark a small fixed resistor with its resistance value coded into three or four color bands.
- Variable resistors are commonly called **potentiometers** or pots. These resistors are built so that the value of resistance can be varied.

THE ELECTRIC CIRCUIT

- An electrical circuit has a voltage source, a load, and a path for the current to flow between the source and the load.
- A **schematic diagram** shows the electrical connections of a circuit. It uses a wide range of symbols to indicate its parts.
- A **pictorial diagram** shows the general physical appearance of the circuit components.
- A **closed circuit** is a circuit where the current has a complete path through which to flow.
- An **open circuit** is a circuit where the path is broken and no current can flow.
- A **switch** is a device used for controlling the flow of current by creating an open or a closed circuit.
- Switch symbols, such as SPST (single-pole--single-throw), are used extensively on schematic drawings.
- Current is measured by an instrument called an ammeter.
- An ammeter is connected so that the measured current must flow through the meter.
- Voltage is measured by a voltmeter.
- The voltmeter is connected across the component for which the voltage measurement is required.
- Resistance is measured with an ohmmeter.
- An ohmmeter is connected across the resistor after the resistor is disconnected from the circuit.
- Most measurements of V, I, and R are made with a combination meter called a VOM (volt-ohm meter) or a DMM (digital multimeter).

TECHNICIAN TIPS

- A voltage source, such as a battery, is nothing more than a large quantity of free electrons chemically forced to one terminal and anxious to find a place to go. Since they repel each other, when a path is available they move along the conductor to the other terminal, which is short of electrons. This movement of electrons is called current. If there is not a complete path between the negative side of the source and the positive side of the source, then no current can flow. This concept is very important: No path--no current.

- In a circuit, when one electron leaves the negative side of a source and enters the wire, another electron leaves the wire at the other end and enters the battery's other terminal. Thus, the movement of an electron occurs along the entire path at the same instant (like a freight train), through the load, and back to the positive side of the source. This means that the current flow is the same anywhere along the path: One path--one current everywhere in the path.

- A load is the useful part of a circuit where the energy from the source is used up or dissipated. There are all kinds of loads, such as motors, heaters, fans, lights, and TVs. The load we will use most in electronics is the resistor. Remember, it is of little use to have a source and a path if nothing is done with the current. Loads are where current does some work.

- The resistor color code is an essential tool for the electronic technician. With this color code, one can tell the resistance value of resistance. It is common to have a simple mnemonic or word association that can help you remember the color values. The following is one example of a mnemonic phrase.

Number	**Color**	**Mnemonic**
0	Black	Bad
1	Brown	Boys
2	Red	Rope
3	Orange	Our
4	Yellow	Young
5	Green	Girls
6	Blue	But
7	Violet	Violet
8	Gray	Goes
9	White	Willingly

- When measuring the voltage across a source or a load, place the black or negative lead at the negative side of the circuit. The positive or red lead will then be placed at the point that you wish to measure. If your meter indicates negative, then you have the leads reversed. Correct them and proceed.

- Current is measured by forcing the current through the meter. This is done by opening or breaking the circuit and then completing the path through the meter leads to the meter and back to the circuit. Be sure to observe the correct polarity, that is, red lead toward the positive and black lead toward the negative side of the source.

- An ohmmeter is used by placing the meter across the resistance or load you wish to measure. Be sure that the power is off AND that one end of the resistor is removed from the circuit before measuring.

CHAPTER 2 QUIZ

Student Name____

1. The movement of free electrons along a conductor is called voltage.
   a. true
   b. false

2. Electrons repel each other.
   a. true
   b. false

3. A resistor color coded with bands of red, red, orange, has a value of 2.2 kΩ.
   a. true
   b. false

4. A DPST switch can open and close two circuits at a time.
   a. true
   b. false

5. To measure the current through a resistor, you place the ammeter across the resistor.
   a. true
   b. false

6. A conductor is a material that has
   a. few free electrons.
   b. a positive charge.
   c. many free electrons.
   d. a structure similar to semiconductors.

7. A material with few free electrons is known as
   a. a conductor.
   b. an insulator.
   c. a semiconductor.

8. A resistor color coded with yellow, violet, red, and silver bands has a value and tolerance of
   a. 47 MΩ +/- 10%
   b. 4.7 kΩ +/- 5%
   c. 4700 Ω +/- 5%
   d. 0.0047 MΩ +/- 10%

9. A resistor has a value of 1.2 Ω +/- 5%. It will be coded
   a. brown, black, red, gold.
   b. brown, black, silver, gold.
   c. brown, black, gold, silver.
   d. brown, black, gold, gold.

10. A resistor has a value of 5.1 MΩ +/- 10%. It will be coded
   a. green, black, blue, silver.
   b. green, brown, blue, silver.
   c. green, brown, green, gold.
   d. green, brown, green, silver.

11. A resistor is color coded with orange, orange, red, gold. Its value and upper and lower tolerance limits are
   a. 3300 Ω, 3135-3465 Ω
   b. 3300 Ω, 2970-3630 Ω
   c. 3300 Ω, 2640-3960 Ω
   d. 3300 Ω, +/- 10%

12. A resistor has a value of 0.47 Ω +/-5%. Its color bands are
   a. violet, yellow, gold, gold.
   b. yellow, violet, gold, gold.
   c. yellow, violet, silver, silver.
   d. yellow, violet, silver, gold.

13. A definition of resistance is
   a. the ability to store a charge.
   b. the opposition to the flow of current.
   c. the movement of free electrons.
   d. the potential difference across a source.

14. When a source is connected to a circuit with an open in it,
   a. the current flow is maximum.
   b. the resistance of the circuit is very low.
   c. the voltage is high.
   d. the current is zero.

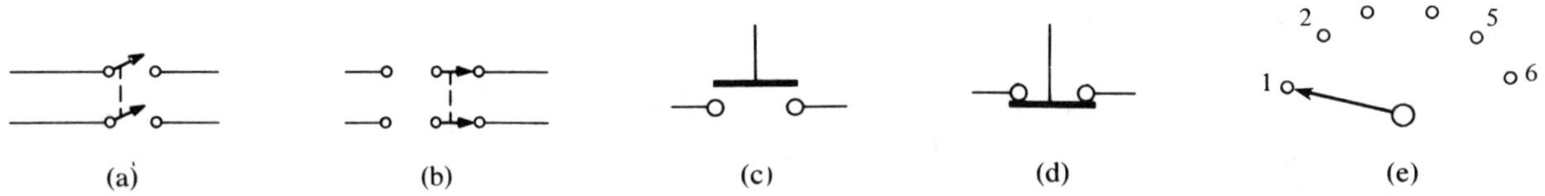

FIGURE 2-1

15. In Figure 2-1, identify the DPST switch.
    a. A
    b. B
    c. C
    d. D
    e. E

16. In Figure 2-1, identify the normally closed push button switch.
    a. A
    b. B
    c. C
    d. D
    e. E

17. In Figure 2-1, identify the DPDT switch.
    a. A
    b. B
    c. C
    d. D
    e. E

18. A complete basic electrical circuit consists of
    a. a source, a load, and a resistor.
    b. a battery, a resistor, and a capacitor.
    c. a source, a load, and a path.
    d. a battery, a path, and a switch.

19. In order to measure the current in a circuit, the ammeter
    a. must be placed across the load.
    b. must be placed so the current must pass through the meter.
    c. must be placed across the source.
    d. should not be used. A voltmeter is the correct instrument.

20. The most common type of diagram used in electronic work is
    a. a pictorial diagram.
    b. a wiring diagram.
    c. a schematic diagram.
    d. a three-view diagram.

REVIEW OF KEY POINTS IN CHAPTER 3

OHM'S LAW AND POWER

OHM'S LAW

- **Ohm's law** shows the relationships that voltage (V), resistance (R), and current (I) have in any circuit.
- The formula for calculating any value of V, I, and R when any two of them are known is I = V/R.
- If the resistance in a circuit remains constant, then an increase in the applied voltage will cause the current to increase.
- Current and voltage are directly proportional.
- If the voltage applied to a circuit remains constant, then an increase in resistance will cause a decrease in the current.
- Current and resistance are inversely proportional.
- If the current remains constant in a circuit, then an increase in resistance will cause an increase in the voltage across a load.
- Voltage and resistance are directly proportional.
- The three versions of the Ohm's law formula are
  I = V/R   V = IR   R = V/I
- The units of V, I, and R, that is, volts, amps, and ohms come out automatically with the Ohm's law formula. Amps = volts/ohms, ohms = volts/amps, and volts = amps x ohms.

POWER

- **Power** is the rate at which energy is used.
- The unit of power (P) is the **watt** (W).
- Power in an electrical circuit is seen as the heat given off by current passing through a resistor.
- The basic power formula is P = VI.

- A variation of the power formula is $P = I^2R$.
- Another variation is $P = V^2/R$.
- Use the correct power formula depending upon the known quantities that you have.

RESISTOR POWER RATINGS

- The power rating of a resistor is dependent on the area of the resistor exposed to the surrounding air.
- The larger the power rating, the greater the physical size of the resistor.
- Standard resistor power rating sizes are 1/8 W, 1/4 W, 1/2 W, 1 W, and 2 W.
- Never use a resistor in an application requiring more power dissipation than the resistor's rating. (Regardless of its rating, the resistor will be too hot to touch).
- The power into a resistor will burn or shorten the life of a resistor if that power is greater than its power rating.

TECHNICIAN TIPS

- To use Ohm's law, you must know two of the three factors. Determine what you have, such as current and voltage. Then look at the version of the law that contains I and V and solve for the resistance. $R = V/I$. Sometimes a simple symbol as shown in Figure 3-1 can be used to make it easier for you.
- To use Figure 3-1, cover up the quantity that you want to find, then the uncovered portion tells you how to proceed. For example, you know V and I and you want to find the resistance. Cover up the R with your finger and you have V/I. This is the correct version of the Ohm's law formula. This circle can be used for any three-element formula, such as the power formulas.

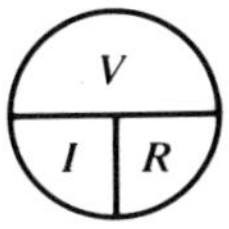

FIGURE 3-1

- If the resistance of a circuit increases, the current will decrease. This is an important fact to remember. Many troubleshooting problems can be solved using this simple Ohm's law relationship. A problem might be that the circuit's current is much higher than it should be. Why? Perhaps the resistance has decreased.

- An increase in voltage across a device will cause the current through the device to increase. This is also an important tool in finding circuit problems. For example, many faults in a transistor amplifier can be found by measuring just three voltages and applying Ohm's law to determine the probable problem.

- Power can be easy to understand. A simple way to look at power is to remember what it is not. Power is not voltage. Power is not current. Power is the product of voltage and current. When current passes through any load, power is dissipated or used up. Lightbulbs are a load that uses power. Most of the power output of a lightbulb is heat, not light. When current flows through a resistor, the product is heat. This heat must be removed by the surrounding air. Always replace a defective resistor with one of the same power rating. To put a smaller-rated resistor in a circuit is asking for problems.

- Be sure to disconnect a resistor from its circuit before measuring the resistance. When using an ohmmeter, polarity is not important.

CHAPTER 3 QUIZ

Student Name____

1. Voltage and resistance are inversely proportional.
   a. true
   b. false

2. A circuit consists of a voltage of 12 V and a resistance of 47 Ω. The circuit's current is 0.255 A.
   a. true
   b. false

3. A circuit consists of a voltage of 12 V and a resistance of 47 Ω. The power dissipated by the resistor is 30.6 W.
   a. true
   b. false

4. If the resistance in a circuit decreases, then the current will increase.
   a. true
   b. false

5. A 47Ω resistor has 0.5 mA flowing through it. It is ok to use a resistor with a power rating of 0.25 W.
   a. true
   b. false

6. Resistance and current are
   a. directly proportional.
   b. inversely proportional.
   c. not related.
   d. are similar to voltage.

7. If the voltage across a circuit decreases, then
   a. the current will increase.
   b. the resistance will decrease.
   c. the resistance will increase.
   d. the current will decrease.

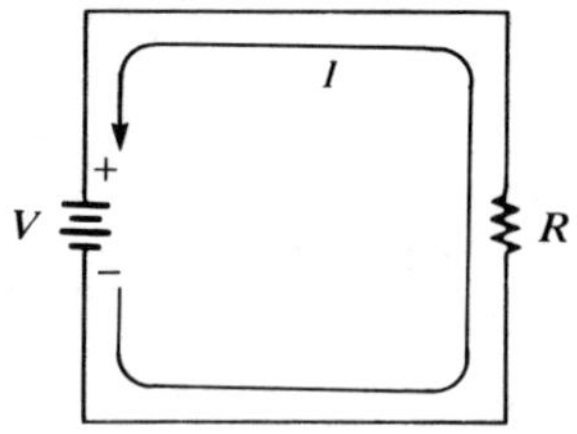

FIGURE 3-2

8. See Figure 3-2. If V = 12 V and R = 23 kΩ, then I =
   a. 0.001 mA
   b. 0.01 mA
   c. 0.1 mA
   d. 1 mA
   e. 10 mA

9. See Figure 3-2. If I = 32 mA and R = 469 Ω, then V =
   a. 12 V
   b. 15 V
   c. 19 V
   d. 22 V

10. See figure 3-2. If V = 67 V and I = 47 mA, then R =
   a. 1.425 kΩ
   b. 1.67 kΩ
   c. 0.70 kΩ
   d. 3.15 Ω

11. See Figure 3-2. If V = 12 V and R = 12 kΩ and the resistor opens, the current will be
   a. 1 mA
   b. hard to determine
   c. 0
   d. 10 mA

12. See Figure 3-2. If the voltage is increased in 1-V steps,
   a. the current will decrease in steps.
   b. the resistance will decrease in steps.
   c. the current will increase in steps.
   d. the resistance and current will not change.

13. See Figure 3-2. If V = 50 V and I = 0.5 mA, then the power dissipated by the resistor is
   a. 25 W
   b. 2.5 W
   c. 0.25 W
   d. 25 mW

14. See Figure 3-2. If V = 50 V and I = 5 A, then the resistor must be capable of dissipating
   a. 250 W
   b. 10 W
   c. 1 W
   d. 250 mW

15. A circuit consisting of a resistor color coded red, red, red is placed across a source of 12 V. What value resistor and wattage rating could be used?
   a. 22000 Ω at 1/4 W
   b. 2200 Ω at 1/2 W
   c. 22 kΩ at 1/4 W
   d. 220 Ω at 1/8 W

16. Which of the following terms is <u>not</u> a resistor rating?
   a. resistor value in ohms
   b. resistor tolerance
   c. current
   d. power rating

17. See Figure 3-2. V = 12 V and R has the color codes brown, black, orange. You measure the current in the circuit. What limits of current might you expect to measure?
   a. 1.2 mA and 1.4 mA
   b. 1 mA and 1.6 mA
   c. 0.8 mA and 1.2 mA
   d. 1 mA and 1.5 mA

18. See Figure 3-2. The resistor is very hot to touch. What should you do to remedy the problem? The current is correct.
   a. Increase the voltage.
   b. Put in a resistor with a smaller value.
   c. Replace the resistor with one of a larger power rating.
   d. Wait for it to burn out and then fix it.

19. A 40-W lightbulb has a resistance measurement of 24 Ω when out of the circuit. What is the resistance of the bulb when it is hot and in a circuit with a supply of 120 V?
   a. 180 Ω
   b. 0.003 Ω
   c. 360 Ω
   d. 1200 Ω

20. See Figure 3-2. If the resistor develops an open,
   a. the power dissipated will increase
   b. the circuit current will decrease.
   c. the source voltage will decrease to zero.
   d. the resistance will decrease.

REVIEW OF KEY POINTS IN CHAPTER 4

SERIES CIRCUITS

RESISTORS IN SERIES

- Resistors in series are connected end-to-end so that all current flows through all of the resistors.
- A series circuit provides only one path for current between any two points of a circuit.
- Look carefully at a schematic diagram and follow the current path from the negative toward the positive. If any resistors are in this path and they have the exact same current through them, then they are in a series.
- If there is only one path, the circuit is series no matter how scrambled the circuit is.
- An ammeter can be placed anywhere in a series circuit to measure the current.

TOTAL SERIES RESISTANCE

- The total resistance of a series circuit is the sum of the individual resistances.
- This can be expressed by $R_T = R_1 + R_2 + R_3 + \ldots + R_n$
- Ohm's law can be used for any device in a series circuit, such as $V_{R1} = I \times R_1$.

SOURCES IN SERIES

- Many voltage sources can be placed in a series circuit.
- To find the total voltage of a group of voltage sources in series, add all the positive sources and subtract all the negative sources.

- Sources in series are called series aiding if their polarities are plus (+) to minus (-).

- Sources in series are called series opposing if their polarities are minus to minus or plus to plus.

KIRCHHOFF'S VOLTAGE LAW

- The difference of potential that appears across a resistance when current flows through it is called a **voltage drop.**

- Kirchhoff's law states that the sum of the individual voltage drops in any closed loop must equal the source voltage.

- In a formula, this is $V_5 = V_{R1} + V_{R2} + V_{R3} + \ldots + V_{Rn}$.

- A series circuit with more than one resistor is a voltage divider; that is, this series circuit divides the source voltage into individual voltage drops across each resistor which can be used for certain applications.

- Ohm's law can be used to find voltage drops in a circuit.

- A shortcut is to use the voltage divider formula. For a series circuit with two resistors in series, $V_{R1} = (R_1/R_T)V_S$. The other values can be found similarly.

- The variable resistor or pot can be used as a voltage divider.

POWER

- The total power dissipated in a series circuit is the sum of the individual powers. The formula is $P_T = P_1 + P_2 + P_3 + \ldots + P_n$

OPENS AND SHORTS

- An open in a series circuit prevents any current from flowing.

- If no current is flowing, then there is no voltage across any resistor in the series circuit.

- There will be a voltage equal to the source across an open resistor.

- A short across the terminals of a resistor will remove that resistance from the circuit, and the total resistance will decrease.

TECHNICIAN TIPS

- In a series circuit there can be only one path for the current to flow. Any resistors in that path must be in series with every other resistor. The total resistance of these resistors in series can be found by adding their values together. For example, a 10 Ω and a 20 Ω resistor are in series. They could be replaced by one 30 Ω resistor. The resistance of an unknown resistor in series can be calculated if you rearrange the series resistance formula to find the unknown value.

$$R_X = R_T - (R_1 + R_2 + R_3)$$

- A series circuit has one current; therefore, the current will be the same anywhere along the path. $I_T = I_1 = I_2 = I_3 = \ldots = I_n$

- Kirchhoff's voltage law is useful because you can find the voltage drops across any resistor in a circuit by applying this law. If $V_S = 12$ V and $V_2 = 3$ V in a series circuit with two resistors, then subtract, $V_1 = V_S - V_2$, or 12 V - 3 V = 9 V.

- There is no reason for a manufacturer of some piece of electronic equipment to connect two or more resistors in series except to divide the voltage and use it somewhere else in the circuit.

- A potentiometer is often used as an adjustable voltage divider. Connect one end or terminal to the source voltage and the other end to ground. The wiper or middle terminal will have a varying voltage between it and ground when the pot is turned.

- If you measure the voltage across a resistor in a series circuit that you think has current flowing through it and the meter reads zero volts, then there is probably an open somewhere in the circuit. Move your meter to read the drop across each resistor until you get the source voltage reading. The open resistor is that one.

- A positive indication of zero current is a zero voltage drop across a resistor. This will become a great troubleshooting tool for you. Remember it.

CHAPTER 4 QUIZ

Student Name ____

1. In a series circuit, the sum of the individual resistor currents equals the total current.
   a. true
   b. false

2. The sum of the individual voltage drops in a series circuit equals the source voltage. This is Kirchhoff's voltage law.
   a. true
   b. false

3. The total power used in a series circuit is the product of each individual resistor's power.
   a. true
   b. false

4. Three resistors, 4.7 kΩ, 1.2 kΩ and 3.3 kΩ are in series. The total resistance is 9200 Ω.
   a. true
   b. false

5. A 1/2-W resistor can safely dissipate more than 1/2 W.
   a. true
   b. false

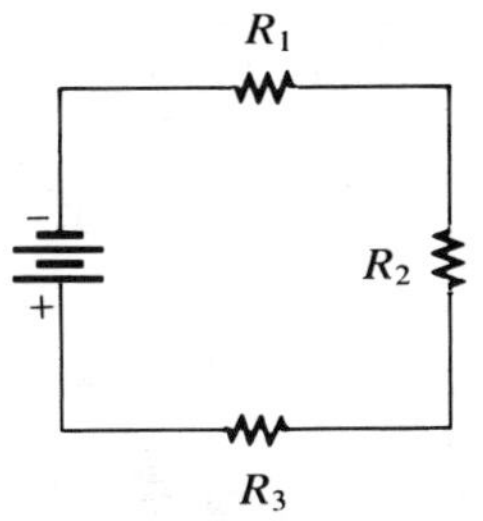

FIGURE 4-1

6. See Figure 4-1. R_1 = 12 kΩ, R_2 = 4.7 kΩ, and R_3 = 2.2 kΩ. R_T =
   a. 19.8 kΩ
   b. 18.9 kΩ
   c. 8.6 kΩ
   d. 1.33 kΩ

7. See Figure 4-1. If R_3 opens and the source voltage is 12 V, the current is
   a. 12 V
   b. maximum
   c. 0
   d. cannot be determined

8. See Figure 4-1. R_1 = 12 kΩ, R_2 = 4.7 kΩ, R_3 = 2.2 kΩ, and V_S = 50 V. The current is
   a. 26.5 mA
   b. 378 mA
   c. 0
   d. 2.65 mA

9. Refer to problem 8. V_{R1} is
   a. 31.8 V
   b. 63.6 V
   c. 5.8 V
   d. 12.4 V

10. Refer to problem 8. V_{R2} is
   a. 16.4 V
   b. 31.8 V
   c. 12.4 V
   d. 5.8 V

11. Refer to problem 8. If R_2 shorts, the voltage drop across R_1 will
   a. increase
   b. decrease
   c. remain the same

12. Refer to problem 8. If R_3 opens, the voltage drop across R_2 will be
   a. 16.5 V
   b. 33.5 V
   c. 9 V
   d. 0 V

13. Refer to problem 8. The total power dissipated in the circuit is
   a. 132.5 mW
   b. 132.5 W
   c. 84 mW
   d. 33 mW

14. Refer to problem 8. If R_1 is shorted out, the total power dissipated by the circuit will
   a. increase
   b. decrease
   c. remain the same

15. Two power supplies are in series with voltages of 12 V and 17 V respectively. What is the total supply voltage?
   a. 5 V
   b. -5 V
   c. 29 V
   d. -29 V

16. Two resistors are in series across a source of 20 V. Each resistor has a value of 100 kΩ. What is the voltage across each resistor?
   a. 20 V
   b. 10 V
   c. 100 mA
   d. 100 kΩ

17. A two-resistor voltage divider has R_1 = 22 kΩ and R_2 = 12 kΩ across 47 V. What is the voltage across R_2?
   a. about 16.6 V
   b. about 30.4 V
   c. about 25.6 V
   d. about 17.2 V

18. A 500 kΩ pot is connected across 5 V. The voltage from the wiper to the lower end of the pot is 1.2 V. What is the resistance of the lower part of the pot?
   a. 380 kΩ
   b. 120 kΩ
   c. 500 kΩ
   d. 0 Ω

19. Three batteries are in series with potentials of 1.2 V, 5 V, and 6 V, but the 1.2-V battery is opposing the other two. The total supply voltage is
   a. 12.2 V
   b. 9.8 V
   c. 1.2 V
   d. 1.3 V

20. Three sources are connected in series aiding. Each has a potential of 8 V. What is the total circuit voltage?
   a. 32 V
   b. 24 V
   c. 16 V
   d. 8 V

REVIEW OF KEY POINTS IN CHAPTER 5

PARALLEL CIRCUITS

RESISTORS IN PARALLEL

- If two or more components are connected across the same voltage source, they are in parallel.
- Each parallel path is called a **branch**.
- If two or more branches share the same voltage, then the branches are in parallel.
- Parallel circuits can be drawn many ways. Follow each current path between two junctions to find the branches that may be in parallel.

VOLTAGES IN PARALLEL CIRCUITS

- The voltage across any parallel branch or component is the same for each branch in parallel.
- This can be stated $V_S = V_1 = V_2 = V_3 = \ldots = V_n$

KIRCHHOFF'S CURRENT LAW

- The sum of the current into a junction equals the sum of the currents out of the junction.
- If there are two branches, then $I_T = I_1 + I_2$.
- When these two currents combine at the junction at the other end of the parallel branch, then $I_1 + I_2 = I_T$.

PARALLEL RESISTORS

- Each time a resistor is added in parallel to a parallel circuit, the total current increases. This means that the total resistance must decrease.
- The total resistance of resistors in parallel is always smaller than the smallest resistor in parallel.

- The formula for resistors in parallel is easy to calculate using a calculator.
- The product over sum method is useful for two resistors in parallel. $R_T = R_1R_2/(R_1 + R_2)$
- Resistors of equal value in parallel can easily be calculated by R_T = R/number of resistors in parallel.

OHM'S LAW IN PARALLEL CIRCUITS

- Ohm's law can be applied to each resistor or to the total circuit values, such as $V_{R1} = I_1R_1$ or $V_S = I_TR_T$.

POWER

- The power dissipated by resistors in parallel is the sum of the individual powers.
- Four 100-W lightbulbs in parallel dissipates 400 W.
- Most house wiring of appliances and lamps are in parallel.
- If one lamp of a parallel circuit burns out, then the others remain lit.

TROUBLES

- If one branch of a parallel circuit opens, then the total resistance increases, and the total current decreases.
- If one branch of a parallel circuit opens, the current in the remaining branches will remain the same.
- If one branch of a parallel circuit shorts, then the entire circuit is shorted. This will cause extreme current to flow, damaging the circuit or blowing the fuse.

TECHNICIAN TIPS

- To determine if resistors are in parallel, draw the current paths from the negative side of the source back to the positive side. Any place a branch occurs, there is a parallel circuit. Carefully follow the two branches and see where the currents come back together. All components of each branch together are in parallel with the components, together, of each other branch. Remember, trace the current paths.

- When you have determined that two or more components are in parallel, then remember the voltage across each of them is the same. In a series circuit, the current is constant. In a parallel circuit, the voltage is constant. If you know the voltage across one parallel branch, you know the voltages across all the branches.

- The current into a junction equals the current out of the junction. This is Kirchhoff's current law. This means you can calculate the current into a two-branch junction by knowing the individual branch currents. Any combination of currents can be calculated by this means.

- Remember, current and resistance are inversely proportional. If any branch opens, then the total current will decrease and the total resistance will increase. Use of this relationship will be of value to developing your troubleshooting skills. You will become so familiar with these relationships that you will start to "think electronics" instead of just doing calculations.

- When applying Ohm's law to a parallel circuit, be sure that you keep the subscripts separate. Use the values for each resistor to calculate any Ohm's law formula for that resistor. Do not mix up values for R_2 with values for R_4 and expect correct answers. Apply Ohm's law to a single resistor or to the total circuit values. Do not mix them. For example, $V_T = I_T R_T$, not $V_T = I_{R7} R_4$.

CHAPTER 5 QUIZ

Student Name ______________________________

1. Four resistors are connected in parallel. The voltage across one resistor is 14 V. The voltage across the other resistors will also be 14 V.
   a. true
   b. false

2. The sum of the values of four resistors in parallel equals the total resistance.
   a. true
   b. false

3. A parallel branch has 1.2 mA flowing. The other branch has 3.4 mA. The total current into the junction of these branches is 4.6 mA.
   a. true
   b. false

4. If an open occurs in one branch of a parallel circuit, then the total current will increase.
   a. true
   b. false

5. The total power dissipated in a parallel circuit is the sum of the individual powers.
   a. true
   b. false

6. A circuit of three parallel resistors, 1.2 kΩ, 4.7 kΩ, and 6.8 kΩ is supplied with a 20-V source. What is the total resistance?
   a. 838 Ω
   b. 1200 Ω
   c. 4700 Ω
   d. 6800 Ω
   e. 12,700 Ω

7. Refer to the values of problem 6. The current through the 4.7-kΩ resistor is
   a. 16.7 mA
   b. 4.25 mA
   c. 2.94 mA
   d. 1.57 mA

8. Two resistors are in parallel, 1500 Ω and 5000 Ω. The total resistance of the circuit is
   a. 1500 Ω
   b. 5000 Ω
   c. greater than 5000 Ω
   d. less than 1500 Ω

9. A parallel circuit consisting of R_1 = 100 Ω, R_2 = 500 Ω and R_3 has an R_T = 77.92 Ω. Find the value of R_3.
   a. 140 Ω
   b. 1200 Ω
   c. 1850 Ω
   d. cannot compute, not enough data

10. A parallel circuit consists of R_1 = 1.2 kΩ in parallel with R_2. I_T = 5 μA and I_2 = 3 μA. What is the value of V_{R1}?
    a. 6 mV
    b. 18 mV
    c. 3.6 mV
    d. 2.4 mV

11. Three resistors are connected in parallel across 50 V. The values are 680 kΩ, 0.047 MΩ and 470 kΩ. If the 0.047-MΩ resistor opens, the total current, I_T, will be
    a. 1.2 mA
    b. 555 μA
    c. 180 μA
    d. 790 μA

12. Six 1.2-MΩ resistors are connected in parallel across 12 V. What is the total resistance of the circuit?
    a. 1.2 MΩ
    b. 250 kΩ
    c. 200 kΩ
    d. 120 kΩ

13. Three parallel branches have a total current of 45 μA flowing into them. I_1 = 15 μA and I_2 = 19 μA. Find the current in the third branch.
    a. 34 μA
    b. 26 μA
    c. 30 μA
    d. 11 μA

14. As resistors are added in parallel to a circuit,
    a. I_T decreases and R_T increases.
    b. I_T decreases and R_T decreases.
    c. I_T increases and R_T decreases.
    d. I_T increases and R_T increases.

15. If a resistor in parallel opens, the total current will
    a. increase and the voltage will decrease.
    b. decrease and the voltage will be constant.
    c. increase and the fuse will blow.
    d. decrease and the voltage will increase.

16. The total power in a parallel circuit
    a. is the sum of the individual powers.
    b. is found by V_T/I_T.
    c. is the sum of the individual powers minus the total power.
    d. is found by $I_1^2R_1$.

17. A circuit consists of three resistors in parallel, R_1 = 4.7 kΩ, R_2 = 3.3 kΩ, and R_3. I_T = 35 mA and V_S = 50 V. Find I_{R3}.
    a. 10.64 mA
    b. 15.15 mA
    c. 9.21 mA
    d. 4.72 mA

18. 680 mA flow into four parallel resistors. The currents through three of the resistors are 95 mA, 400 mA, 19 mA. The current through the fourth resistor is
    a. 585 mA
    b. 280 mA
    c. 261 mA
    d. 166 mA

19. Two resistors are in parallel. R_1 = 470 Ω and R_T = 330 Ω. Find the value of R_2.
    a. 770 Ω
    b. 1108 Ω
    c. 194 Ω
    d. 110 Ω

20. House wiring of lamps are usually in parallel
    a. so they will draw less current.
    b. because the resistance is higher.
    c. so one lamp burnout will not affect the other lamps.
    d. because the power is greater than in a series circuit.

REVIEW OF KEY POINTS IN CHAPTER 6

SERIES-PARALLEL CIRCUITS

SERIES-PARALLEL CIRCUITS

- A series-parallel or combination circuit consists of many resistances, some in series and some in parallel.
- Look carefully at the current paths. If the same current flows through several resistors, then they are all in series. If there is a current branch, then there is a parallel circuit.
- It is common for parts of circuits to be in parallel with other parts, or in series with other parts.
- Start at the negative side of the source following the current path. If the same current passes through any resistors in that path, then those resistors are in series.
- When you come to a branch, whatever resistors that are in each part of that branch are in parallel with the other branch. Each branch may contain series resistors.
- Sometimes combination circuits are drawn so that it is difficult to see the series and parallel combinations. Redrawing the circuit will often make it easy to see the combinations.
- If you can see the combinations, then you can easily calculate values and analyze the circuit.

CALCULATING SERIES-PARALLEL CIRCUITS

- You must be able to see the combinations, either series or parallel. If you see a series combination, then apply series circuit rules to solve that part of the circuit.
- If you see a parallel combination, then apply parallel rules to solve that part of the circuit.
- You will be changing your thinking from series to parallel and back as often as required to solve any combination circuit.

- Find the equivalent value of resistors in series or parallel and redraw the circuit. Work in stages.
- Remember, branches in parallel have the same voltage across them. This is true even if the branches contain complex networks.
- Remember, resistors in series share the same current, and resistors in parallel share the same voltage.

REFERENCE POINTS

- In a circuit a common reference point is usually called ground.
- This ground is often at the negative side of the voltage source.
- The reference point called **ground** has a potential of zero volts with respect to all other parts of the circuit.
- Voltage measurements are often taken with respect to ground. This means that the voltmeter leads are attached to ground and the point to be measured.
- Subscripts are often used to denote a particular voltage. If a point is labeled A and another point is called B, then the voltage between points A and B is $V_{AB} = V_A - V_B$. Each voltage V_A and V_B is measured with respect to ground.

VOLTAGE DIVIDERS

- Two or more resistors in series form a voltage divider. If a load is connected across one resistor of a voltage divider, then a series-parallel circuit exists and the voltage divider is then "loaded."
- Series-parallel calculation rules apply to a loaded voltage divider.
- The natural result of loading a voltage divider is a lowering of the voltage at the load terminals.
- Voltmeters have a high internal resistance so that little loading effect is done when measuring across a load.

- Voltage dividers can have voltages above and below ground potential.

CIRCUIT THEOREMS

- Circuits with more than one voltage source can be solved by use of the superposition method. Short each source one at a time, then solve for the unknown current in each case with a different source shorted. Combine these currents to find the total unknown current.

- Thevenin's theorem allows you to substitute an equivalent, two-component circuit and solve for the unknown values, using the simpler Thevenin's circuit.

- A Wheatstone bridge circuit is often used in sensitive measuring circuits to determine an unknown resistance or voltage.

CIRCUIT FAULTS

- Opens or shorts can occur in series-parallel circuits.

- Voltage measurements, usually with respect to ground, can be made and the trouble isolated by an analysis of such measurements.

- A higher than normal voltage across the parallel portion of a combination circuit could indicate an open in one of the parallel branches.

TECHNICIAN TIPS

- Identifying a series or parallel part of a combination circuit can be simple. Be sure to draw all of the arrows indicating current paths. Start at the negative side of the source. Any resistor that all the current flows through is in series with any other resistor that shares the same current. When you come to a junction, follow the current in each branch until the branches return together. Each branch is then in parallel. Continue around the circuit until you are back at the source.

- In each branch that you found, follow the current to see if any resistors are in series. There may even be additional parallel branches. Once you have identified the series and parallel combinations, you are ready to analyze the circuit.

- If you found series resistors, combine them into one equivalent value and redraw the circuit. If you found resistors in parallel, proceed using parallel combination techniques. Gradually simplify the circuit until only one resistor is left.

- Calculating for total current is then possible. Expand the circuit in the opposite way that you simplified it, gradually finding all of the required values. Remember that resistors in series share the same current and resistors or branches in parallel share the same voltage.

- The use of circuit ground is common in electronic measuring. It is common to connect your black voltmeter lead to ground and the red lead to the point requiring measuring. Remember, the voltage drop across a resistor or load is the difference in the voltage-to-ground measurements from each end of the resistor. For example, $V_{BE} = V_B - V_E$. It is possible for that value to be negative. V_{BE} could be positive or negative depending on the circuit conditions.

- A load applied to a resistor in a voltage divider will always result in a decrease in voltage across that resistor. If a voltmeter is used to measure a voltage across a load, it should have a high internal resistance to avoid loading the circuit under test.

CHAPTER 6 QUIZ

Student Name ______________________________

1. See Figure 6-1. R_2 is in parallel with R_3.
   a. true
   b. false

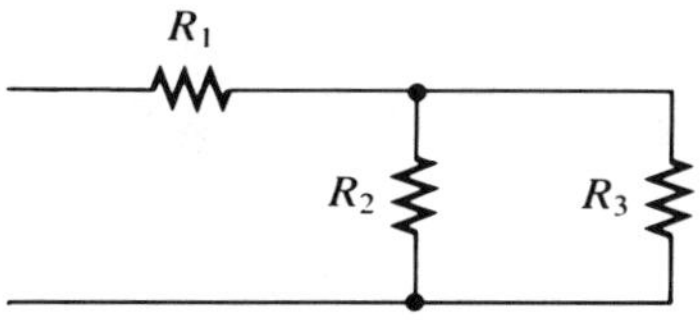

FIGURE 6-1

2. See Figure 6-1. R_1 is in series with R_2.
   a. true
   b. false

3. See Figure 6-1. R_2 is in series with the parallel combination R_1 and R_2.
   a. true
   b. false

4. Resistors are in parallel if they share the same current.
   a. true
   b. false

5. In a combination circuit, the total resistance can be represented by one resistor of the correct value.
   a. true
   b. false

6. See Figure 6-1. Resistor R_1 is connected
   a. in series with R_2.
   b. in series with R_3.
   c. in parallel with R_2.
   d. in parallel with R_3.
   e. none of these

7. See Figure 6-2. R_1 and R_4 are connected
   a. in series with each other and R_3.
   b. in series with each other and R_2 and R_5.
   c. in series with each other.
   d. in parallel with R_3.

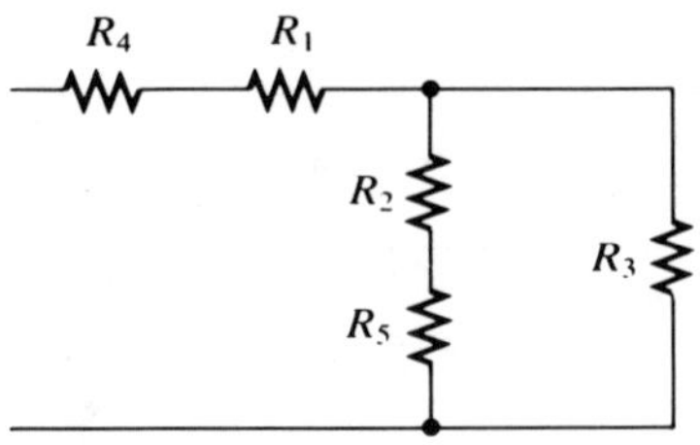

FIGURE 6-2

8. See Figure 6-2. R_2 and R_5 are connected
   a. in series with each other and in parallel with R_3.
   b. in parallel.
   c. in series with R_1.
   d. in series with R_3.

9. See Figure 6-1. If R_1 = 4.7 kΩ, R_2 = 3300 Ω and R_3 = 1000 Ω, the total resistance of the circuit is
   a. 5700 Ω
   b. 5467 Ω
   c. 4125 Ω
   d. 660 Ω

10. See Figure 6-1 and the values in problem 9. If the source voltage is 50 V, calculate the total current.
   a. 8.8 mA
   b. 9.15 mA
   c. 12.1 mA
   d. 75.7 mA

11. Refer to problem 10. The voltage drop across R_3 is
   a. 42.9 V
   b. 5.62 V
   c. 7.01 V
   d. 1.76 V

12. See Figure 6-2. If all of the resistors are 33 kΩ, the total resistance is
   a. 165 kΩ
   b. 55 kΩ
   c. 116.5 kΩ
   d. 88 kΩ

13. See Figure 6-2. If all of the resistors are 1000 Ω and the source voltage is 25 V, the voltage drop across R_3 is
   a. 6.25 V
   b. 43.75 V
   c. 18.75 V
   d. 25 V

14. See Figure 6-1. If another resistor is placed in parallel with R_3,
   a. V_{R1} will decrease.
   b. V_{R2} will decrease.
   c. I_1 will decrease.
   d. I_2 will increase.

15. See Figure 6-3. If V_{R2} = 12 V, find V_{DE}.
   a. -12 V
   b. 12 V
   c. 24 V
   d. 36 V

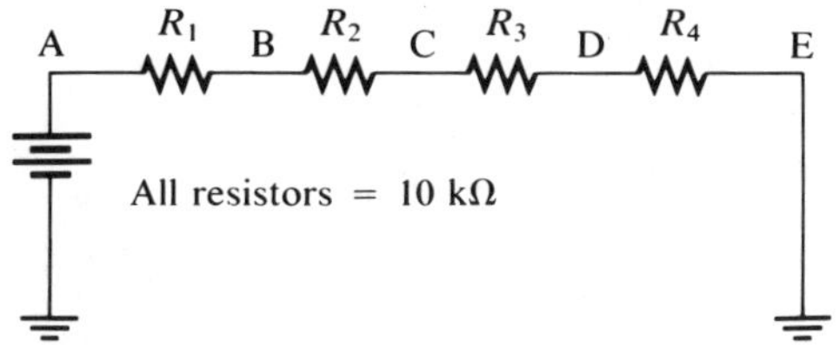

FIGURE 6-3

16. See Figure 6-3. If V_D = 9.6 V, find V_{DB}.
   a. 9.6 V
   b. 4.8 V
   c. 19.2 V
   d. -19.2 V

17. See Figure 6-2. If R_2 shorts, I_5 will
   a. increase.
   b. decrease.
   c. remain the same.

18. See Figure 6-2. If R_3 opens, V_{R4} will
   a. increase.
   b. decrease.
   c. remain the same.

19. See Figure 6-2. If R_4 shorts, V_{R3} will
   a. increase.
   b. decrease.
   c. remain the same.

20. If a combination of four parallel 10-kΩ resistors were in series with a single 20-kΩ resistor, and one of the parallel combination resistors opened, the voltage across the other parallel resistors would
   a. increase.
   b. decrease.
   c. remain the same.

REVIEW OF KEY POINTS IN CHAPTER 7

MAGNETISM AND ELECTROMAGNETISM

MAGNETISM

- All magnets, such as a permanent magnet, create a magnetic field around them.
- The magnetic field is said to leave the north pole of the magnet and travel to the south pole. The return is through the magnet.
- If the like poles (north-north or south-south) of two magnets are placed close to each other, there is a repulsion force causing them to move apart.
- If the unlike poles are placed close to each other, a force exists that will cause the magnets to attract each other.
- If a nonmagnetic material is placed in a magnetic field, the field will pass through it and will not be altered.
- A magnetic material placed in a field will cause the field to intensify through the magnetic material and thus will distort the field.
- Nonmagnetic materials are glass, paper, wood, and humans.
- Magnetic materials are iron, steel, and certain metals.
- Magnetic flux or lines of force are names for the magnetic field.
- Flux density or flux per unit area is a measure of the strength of a magnetic field. The greater the number of lines of force, the stronger the magnet.
- A magnetic material has small magnetic domains in its atomic structure. These domains normally have a random position, but when they are exposed to a magnetic field, they will line up north to south and form a magnet.

ELECTROMAGNETISM

- Any conductor carrying a current has a magnetic field around it. This is the same magnetic field as in a magnet.

- The field around a current-carrying conductor is circular.
- The left-hand rule can be used for determining the direction of the field. Imagine placing your left hand with the thumb in the direction of the electron current. Your fingers will indicate the direction of the field around the conductor.
- **Magnetomotive force** (mmf) is the force that produces a magnetic field around a conductor.
- The unit for mmf is the ampere-turn (At).
- **Permeability** is a measure of the ease of magnetizing a magnetic material. The permeability of air is 1.
- An **electromagnet** is a coil of wire carrying current.
- An electromagnet has a north and south pole and behaves just like a permanent magnet.
- If the current in an electromagnet is reversed, the magnetic field will also reverse.

INDUCTION

- If a conductor is moved through a magnetic field, a voltage is induced in the conductor.
- The amount of voltage produced depends upon the rate of movement through the field, the strength of the field, and the length of the conductor in the field.
- The polarity of the induced voltage depends upon the direction of motion of the conductor through the field.
- A generator for producing direct current is made of a coil of wire rotating in a magnetic field.
- The induced voltage depends upon the relative motion between the field and the conductor. In other words, the conductor does not have to move. The magnetic field can move through a stationary conductor.

TECHNICIAN TIPS

- Relays use electromagnetism for their operation. A coil of wire is energized by a source. The magnetic force created by the current flowing through the coil will cause a set of contacts to close and switch on a circuit. A relay is a device that allows you to control the power supplied to a load from a remote location. There are many types of relays from small ones used on a printed circuit board to giant relays used by the commercial power companies.

CHAPTER 7 QUIZ

Student Name ____

1. A permanent magnet will lose its magnetism quickly.
   a. true
   b. false

2. Unlike magnetic poles have an attraction force between them.
   a. true
   b. false

3. A magnetic field is made of lines of force.
   a. true
   b. false

4. A conductor carrying current has a magnetic field around it.
   a. true
   b. false

5. Relays, alarm systems, and loudspeakers are some uses for magnetism.
   a. true
   b. false

6. A magnetic field can be described by
   a. magnetic flux.
   b. an electrostatic field.
   c. the product of voltage and current.
   d. field intensity.

7. An electromagnet
   a. has opposite poles than a permanent magnet.
   b. is created when a current stops flowing.
   c. has north and south poles.
   d. is effected by light.

8. A coil of wire wound around a core could be called
   a. a capacitor.
   b. a solenoid.
   c. a burglar alarm.
   d. a permanent magnet.

9. Two permanent bar magnets are brought close to each other.
   a. They will attract if the two north poles are together.
   b. They will attract if the two south poles are together.
   c. They will repel if the north and south poles are together.
   d. They will attract if the north and south poles are together.

10. The quantity of lines of force per unit of area is known as
    a. magnetic flux.
    b. ampere-turns.
    c. flux density.
    d. permeability.

11. The ease of a material to be magnetized is called
    a. permeability.
    b. the shielding effect.
    c. reluctance.
    d. induction.

12. Magnetic lines of force are said to
    a. leave the south pole and enter the north pole.
    b. leave the north pole and enter the south pole.
    c. always travel clockwise.
    d. always travel counter-clockwise.

13. If a conductor is moved through a magnetic field,
    a. a voltage will be produced.
    b. a magnetic field will be produced.
    c. permeability will be increased.
    d. the reluctance will decrease.

14. The strength of an electromagnet depends upon
    a. the temperature.
    b. the core material.
    c. the speed of motion.
    d. the length of the conductor.

15. The voltage produced by a magnetic field cutting a conductor
    a. is dependent on the direction of motion.
    b. is dependent on the speed of motion.
    c. is dependent on the length of the conductor.
    d. is all of the above.

16. Flux density is measured in a unit called a/an
    a. weber
    b. ampere-turn
    c. tesla
    d. maxwell

17. The polarity of an induced voltage depends on
    a. the time of a conductor in a magnetic field.
    b. the length of a conductor in a magnetic field.
    c. the direction of motion of a conductor in a magnetic field.
    d. the amount of current flowing.

18. The magnetic term equivalent to voltage in a circuit is called
    a. reluctance.
    b. magnetomotive force.
    c. flux density.
    d. current.

19. A unit of mmf is called
    a. the weber.
    b. the tesla.
    c. the ampere-turn.
    d. the gauss.

20. The force induced across a coil of wire carrying current could be called
    a. voltage.
    b. mmf.
    c. the ampere-turn.
    d. the weber.

REVIEW OF KEY POINTS IN CHAPTER 8

MEASURING INSTRUMENTS

ANALOG METERS

- An analog-type meter has a needle and a scale upon which the value of current or voltage is calibrated.

- A moving-coil meter operates by a deflection of a current-carrying coil in a magnetic field. The greater the current, the greater the deflection.

- The sensitivity of an analog meter is the amount of current that will produce a full-scale reading.

- An analog ammeter's coil measures the results from the voltage drop across an internal resistor called a shunt. The meter can read different ranges of current by switching various values of shunt resistors.

- The internal resistance of an ammeter's coil and shunt is very low.

- The voltmeter utilizes a movement similar to the ammeter, except a series resistor is added to lower the current to the value of current the meter can handle in the coil. This is called the **multiplier resistance.**

- Various voltage ranges can be measured by switching in various multiplier resistors.

- The internal resistance of a voltmeter should be very high to avoid loading the circuit under test.

- An ohmmeter uses the same movement as the ammeter except a known voltage source and series resistor are built inside the meter and are connected to the circuit under test. The scale is then calibrated in ohms even thought the ohmmeter is actually measuring current. (Now you know why analog ohmmeters have the 0 Ω marking at the full scale reflection point.)

- In use an analog ohmmeter should be adjusted to zero ohms with the leads shorted.

DIGITAL METERS

- Digital multimeters or DMMs are used more that any other kind of measuring instrument today.
- Most DMMs will measure voltage, current, and resistance. Some meters have other special measurement functions.
- The display of a DMM is usually an LED or LCD seven-segment type.
- The accuracy of a DMM is greater than most analog meters.
- Usually, the more digits in the display, the higher the accuracy of the meter.

OSCILLOSCOPE

- The scope is widely used by technicians to measure voltage and time.
- Most scopes have the ability to measure two voltages at one time and are called dual-trace scopes.
- The vertical deflection on the scope's screen represents the voltage at any particular time. It is calibrated and measured by the amount of vertical deflection.
- The horizontal deflection of the trace on the screen is called the time base and is controlled by the internal sweep voltages of the scope. These sweep rates are varied by controls on the scope's front panel.

TECHNICIAN TIPS

- When using an analog meter, carefully line up your eye with the needle. Look at it straight on and at the same level. Some better meters have a mirror behind the needle that can be used to line up the reading. Place your eye so that you cannot see the reflection of the needle in the mirror. You will be in the correct position to read that meter.

- If the voltage or current you are planning to measure is unknown, then always start with the meter in the highest scale. If you see that you will not exceed the next lower scale maximum, then change to that scale. Keep lowering the scale multiplier until you can read towards the maximum part of the scale. You will then have the most accurate reading for that meter.

- Digital multimeters usually have built-in over-voltage or over-current protection. If you read over the scale of the meter, it will indicate an over-range in one of several ways. Learn your meter's over-range indication.

- The oscilloscope or scope is a useful instrument to the electronic technician. Instantaneous voltages can be seen and measured. As with the analog meters, be sure you line up your eye with the trace for the most accurate reading. Another good idea is to make your trace as large as convenient on the screen by adjusting the vertical control. This will help ensure an accurate reading.

- Learn to use the scope controls properly. If you do not see a trace on the screen, carefully analyze your circuit, connections, or scope settings. Then adjust the controls to get your trace. Do not become a knob turner, turning every knob on the scope with the hope you will finally get a trace on the screen. Learn the scope.

CHAPTER 8 QUIZ

Student Name ____

1. A voltmeter should have a low internal resistance.
   a. true
   b. false

2. An ammeter is placed in series with the current you want to measure.
   a. true
   b. false

3. Generally, digital meters are not as accurate as analog meters.
   a. true
   b. false

4. The horizontal deflection on an oscilloscope measures time.
   a. true
   b. false

5. The most accurate meter to read dc voltages is the scope.
   a. true
   b. false

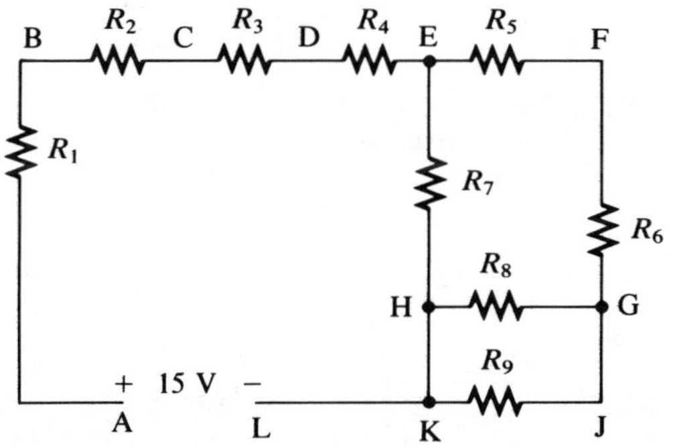

FIGURE 8-1

6. See Figure 8-1. If you place the red lead of a voltmeter on point F and the black lead on point G, you will read
   a. V_{R5}
   b. I_{R5}
   c. V_{R8}
   d. V_{R6}

7. See Figure 8-1. To measure the current through R_3, the circuit must be opened and the meter placed at point
   a. A
   b. E
   c. J
   d. H

8. See Figure 8-1. Voltmeter leads placed across points E and G will read
   a. V_{R6}
   b. V_{R4}
   c. $V_{R7} + V_{R8}$
   d. V_{R7}

9. See Figure 8-1. To determine the power dissipated in R_3, you would
   a. measure the voltage from points C to D and calculate the power.
   b. measure the current at point E, the voltage across R_3, and calculate the power.
   c. measure the current at point C, the voltage across R_3, and calculate the power.
   d. use your DMM and measure the power directly.

10. See Figure 8-1. If the circuit opened at point J,
    a. the current at point B would increase.
    b. the current at point D would decrease.
    c. V_{R9} would increase.
    d. I_9 would increase.

11. The vertical deflection of a scope trace is 1.6 cm. The volts/div switch is on 50 mV/cm. The voltage is
    a. 80 mV
    b. 50 mV
    c. 1.6 mV
    d. 0.008 V

12. See Figure 8-1. If the current through R_1 were to be measured, the ammeter would be placed in the circuit at point
    a. A
    b. B
    c. C
    d. any of the above

13. See Figure 8-1. The measured voltage V_{HG} is the same as
    a. V_{R7}
    b. V_{R6}
    c. V_{R5}
    d. V_{R9}

14. See Figure 8-1. If R_2 shorts to the positive side of the source, V_{R1} will
    a. increase.
    b. decrease.
    c. remain the same.

15. See Figure 8-1. If the source voltage were changed to ac, the instrument to measure resistances in this circuit would be
    a. an ohmmeter.
    b. a voltmeter.
    c. an oscilloscope.
    d. an ammeter.

16. Your scope is set up to measure a voltage, but the trace is a straight horizontal line. The problem could be
    a. there is no voltage to the circuit.
    b. the scope is connected to ground.
    c. the input scope switch is set to the ground position.
    d. any of these.

17. Your scope is set up with the time base switch on 20 µs/cm. The trace is 7.5 cm long. What time period does this represent?
    a. 1.5 µs
    b. 5 µs
    c. 150 µs
    d. 0.0015 s

18. When an accurate measurement is desired with a scope,
    a. the trace can be small.
    b. the trace should be large and you should look straight at the trace.
    c. no care is required.
    d. just make the trace large.

19. An analog voltmeter is used to measure a voltage and the meter deflects to the left. This indicates
    a. the meter leads are reversed.
    b. the voltage is too small to be read.
    c. the voltage is too large to be read.
    d. the resistor is in the circuit backwards.

20. To measure resistance,
    a. always measure from negative to positive.
    b. always shut the power off.
    c. always disconnect the resistor from the circuit.
    d. always measure from positive to negative.

REVIEW OF KEY POINTS IN CHAPTER 9

INTRODUCTION TO ALTERNATING CURRENT AND VOLTAGE

ac SINE WAVE

- A sine wave alternates between positive and negative values.
- A sine wave always repeats itself. One complete alternation is called a cycle. The length of time for each cycle is called the **period** (T).
- **Frequency** is the number of cycles that a sine wave completes in a second.
- The unit of frequency (f) is cycles/second or hertz (Hz).
- The period is the reciprocal of the frequency. $f = 1/T$, $T = 1/f$.

MEASURING SINE WAVES

- **Instantaneous values** of voltage or current are those values that occur at any particular time during the sine wave.
- The **peak value** of a sine wave is that value at either the positive or negative peak of the wave form.
- The **peak-to-peak value** is the voltage between the positive and negative peaks. For example, +10 volts to -10 volts is 20 volts p-p.
- The p-p value is therefore twice the peak value. $V_{p-p} = 2\ V_p$.
- The **rms value** of an ac voltage is equal to the battery voltage that will produce the same amount of power in the same circuit.

$$V_{rms} = 0.707\ V_p$$

SINE WAVE SOURCES

- An ac generator consisting of a coil of wire rotating in a magnetic field will produce a sine wave output.

- The frequency depends upon the speed of rotation of the coil.
- An audio frequency signal generator is an instrument that generates alternating current in electronic circuits. It often includes sine, square, and triangle wave outputs.
- An rf signal generator is an instrument that produces a radio frequency sine wave.

ANGLES AND PHASES

- The angular position of a sine wave may be expressed in radians or more commonly in degrees.
- There are 360° in one cycle of a sine wave. One-half cycle is 180°. One quarter cycle is 90°.
- A sine wave may be shifted in phase. This means that there is a phase or time difference between the start of one cycle compared to the start of the phase-shifted cycle.
- Any instantaneous value (v) of voltage on a sine wave may be calculated by $V = V_p \sin \Theta$. Θ is the angle starting from 0°.
- Phasor or vector diagrams are useful for representing a sine wave in a simple form. To minimize the confusion that results from drawing the many sine waves for the various voltages and currents, phasors are used. Each phasor will then represent a voltage or a current. The relationships are simple right triangles, which are easily solved.

OHM'S LAW AND KIRCHHOFF'S LAW

- Ohm's law works similar to dc values, except that if you use p-p values, then the answer will be in p-p values.
- Kirchhoff's law also works except that the addition of the voltages may not always add directly if simple arithmetic is used. This will be seen in later chapters.

NONSINUSOIDAL WAVEFORMS

- ac waveforms may be in the form of a positive or negative pulse.

- Repetitive pulses or square waves are also ac.
- Triangle and sawtooth waveforms are ac as well.
- All non-sine waveforms have harmonics. This means, for example, that the fundamental frequency of 1 kHz may have a second harmonic frequency of 2 kHz, a third of 3 kHz, and so on, depending upon their shape.

TECHNICIAN TIPS

- Sine waves can be seen and measured on the scope. It will help you to measure accurately if you learn to adjust the trace peaks, either positive or negative, to one of the horizontal lines on the scope screen. Carefully count the divisions and their fractions to the other peak. Then, multiply by the setting on the vertical switch. This value is the peak-to-peak voltage you are measuring. It is difficult to measure the peak voltage on the scope. If you need this reading, measure the p-p and divide it by two to get the peak voltage.
- The scope is an excellent instrument to measure the period of a sine wave, or any other repeating wave. You can move the trace so either the positive or negative peaks are on the center horizontal line. Then measure the distance from the peak of one cycle to the peak of the next cycle. Multiply this by the time base reading and you will have the period in seconds. Invert this value with your calculator and the frequency is on your calculator.
- Phasor diagrams, sometimes called vector diagrams, are a very useful method of representing sine wave values. It is easier to see the phase difference between two voltages with phasors than by trying to draw the sine waves of the two voltages. Always draw the phasor that represents the voltage across or current through a resistor in the horizontal direction and toward the right. The phase angle is then easily seen and in fact ac problems can be solved more easily using phasor diagrams. Phasor diagrams can have both positive and negative values in any of the four quadrants. The most used quadrants are from 270 to 90 degrees.
- Ohm's law and Kirchhoff's law also apply to ac circuits. Just remember that if the values you are using are p-p voltage, then the current you solve for will also be a p-p value. Resistance, of course, is still resistance in an ac circuit.

CHAPTER 9 QUIZ

Student Name ____

1. The period of a sine wave is the reciprocal of the frequency.
   a. true
   b. false

2. The higher the frequency of a sine wave, the longer the period.
   a. true
   b. false

3. The peak value of a sine wave is larger in value than the rms value.
   a. true
   b. false

4. If an ac voltage is applied to a resistor, the current decreases as the voltage increases.
   a. true
   b. false

5. Sine, square, and triangle waves are all forms of ac waves.
   a. true
   b. false

6. The formula for V_{rms} for a sine wave is
   a. V_{p-p} x 0.707
   b. V_p x 0.707
   c. V_p x 1.414
   d. V_{p-p} x 1.414

7. The rms value of a sine wave voltage means
   a. the heating effect of a battery of the same voltage.
   b. the root mean square value.
   c. I_{rms} x R.
   d. all of these.

8. A sine wave has a peak value of 169 V. What is the instantaneous value at an angle of 37°?
   a. 135 V
   b. 119 V
   c. 239 V
   d. 49 V

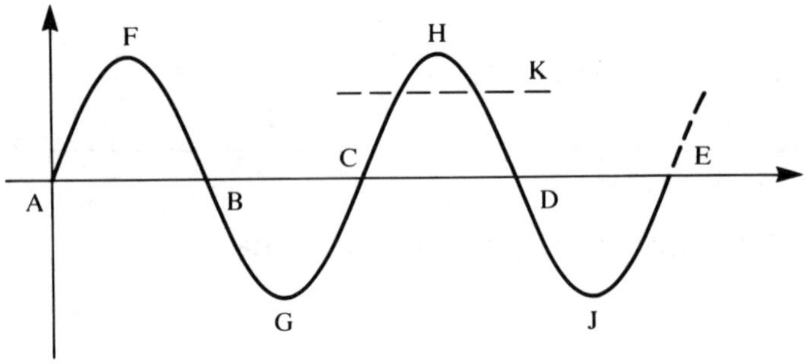

FIGURE 9-1

9. See Figure 9-1. The figure shows
   a. four complete cycles.
   b. four positive and four negative alternations.
   c. two complete cycles.
   d. four positive alternations.
   e. four negative alternations.

10. The number of cycles occurring in one second is called
    a. an alternation.
    b. revolutions per minute.
    c. alternating current.
    d. the frequency.

11. See Figure 9-1. The time from point B to point C is called
    a. an alternation.
    b. a cycle.
    c. the period.
    d. peak voltage.

12. See Figure 9-1. The voltage value at point H represents
    a. rms voltage.
    b. p-p voltage.
    c. peak voltage.
    d. one cycle of voltage.

13. See Figure 9-1. The rms voltage is seen at point
    a. J
    b. K
    c. F
    d. E

14. See Figure 9-1. The time from points G to J is known as
    a. one cycle.
    b. one alternation.
    c. the rms value.
    d. V_p.

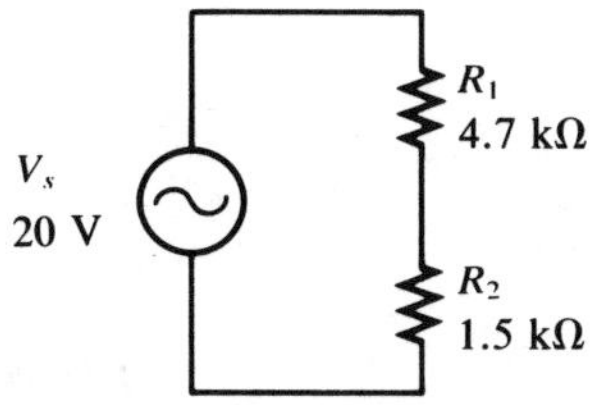

FIGURE 9-2

15. See Figure 9-2. Find V_{R1}.
    a. 15.16 V_{p-p}
    b. 42.88 V_p
    c. 21.43 V_p
    d. 15.16 V_p

16. See Figure 9-2. Find I_{p-p}.
    a. 4.55 mA
    b. 3.22 mA
    c. 9.11 mA
    d. 6.44 mA

17. See Figure 9-2. Find V_{R2p-p}.
    a. 4.84 V
    b. 9.68 V
    c. 13.69 V
    d. 6.84 V

18. The correct formula for finding the period of a sine wave is
    a. T = 1/f
    b. f = 1/T
    c. T = 0.707f
    d. T = 1.414f

19. A square wave has a period of 5 s, and a peak value of 10 V. Determine the rise time of the wave.
    a. 5 s
    b. 200 kHz
    c. 7.07 V
    d. cannot be determined

20. A square wave consists of
    a. a fundamental and even harmonics.
    b. a fundamental and all harmonics.
    c. a fundamental and odd harmonics.
    d. even and odd harmonics only.

REVIEW OF KEY POINTS IN CHAPTER 10

CAPACITORS

CAPACITANCE AND CAPACITORS

- A capacitor consists of two plates separated by an insulator.
- A capacitor stores charge. Charge (Q) is a quantity of electrons.
- As a charge is stored in a capacitor, a voltage is produced across the capacitor.
- The mathematical symbol for capacitance is C.
- The basic formula for the performance of a capacitance is $C = Q/V$.
- The basic unit of capacitance is the farad (F). Common values of capacitance in electronics are μF (10^{-6}) and pF (10^{-12}).
- The voltage rating of a capacitor is the voltage that the insulating or dielectric material can withstand without puncturing.
- All capacitors leak, that is, they will conduct a little amount of current. Some types of capacitors leak more than others.
- The physical characteristics depend upon the following:
  - The area of the plates
  - The distance between the plates
  - The dielectric constant of the insulating material separating the plates

CAPACITOR TYPES

- The dielectric material determines the type of capacitor.
- There are mica, ceramic, paper, mylar, Teflon, and plastic film capacitors.

- A common large value capacitor is the electrolytic. These capacitors have either aluminum or tantalum oxide as dielectric.
- Electrolytic capacitors are polarized and must be in the circuit correctly.
- Radio and TV tuners often use variable capacitors. The dielectric in this case is air.

CAPACITORS IN CIRCUITS

- If capacitors are connected in parallel, the value of capacitance adds. $C_T = C_1 + C_2 + C_3 + \ldots + C_n$
- Capacitors in series combine in a similar fashion as resistors in parallel.
- The smallest series capacitor will have the greatest voltage across it.

CAPACITORS IN dc CIRCUITS

- When a capacitor is connected across a dc supply, the capacitor charges in a nonlinear fashion. The charging current is not constant.
- At the instant the switch closes, connecting the capacitor to the supply, the current in the capacitor circuit is maximum.
- The voltage across an initially discharged capacitor is zero.
- All of the source voltage appears across the series resistor.
- All of the above voltages and current change as the capacitor takes on a charge. The current decreases, the voltage across the capacitor increases and the voltage across the series resistor decreases.
- A time constant is the time it takes any voltage or current to change 63.2%.

- The formula for time constant is $\tau = RC$.

- Once a capacitor is fully charged, the circuit appears to be an open circuit and the current is zero.

CAPACITORS IN ac CIRCUITS

- There is always a phase shift between ac voltage and ac current in a capacitive circuit.

- The current leads the capacitor voltage by 90°.

- A capacitor offers an opposition to the flow of ac current. This is called **capacitive reactance** (X_C). The unit of X_C is the ohm (Ω). The formula for X_C is $X_C = 1/2\pi fC$

- As the ac frequency is increased, the capacitive reactance decreases.

OHM'S LAW AND POWER

- Ohm's law is applied by using X_C as "resistance" is used in a dc circuit. $I_C = V_C/X_C$. The other forms follow similarly.

- True power (P_{true}) is zero because nearly all of the energy stored in a capacitor is returned to the source when the capacitor discharges.

- Reactive power (P_r) is found by applying the power formulas. Substitute X_C for resistance:

$$P_r = I^2_{rms}X_C$$

CAPACITOR USES

- Many amplifiers use capacitors to couple the signal from one stage to another. These are coupling capacitors.

- Capacitors block dc and isolate the various dc voltages in a circuit from each other.

- Power supply filter circuits use electrolytic capacitors to smooth the pulsating dc.

- Bypass capacitors are used to provide an alternate path for an ac signal around a resistor.

- Capacitors are used in tuned circuits to provide frequency selection, as in a radio.

TECHNICIAN TIPS

- Electrolytic capacitors usually have a large value of capacitance. These capacitors are polarized and must be placed in a circuit so the negative side of the capacitor is connected toward the negative side of the circuit and so that they always have some dc voltage across them. If you connect the polarity incorrectly, it is possible for the cap to heat up and explode. This may hurt someone and make a mess to clean up. If you connect an electrolytic backwards, you will probably do so only once. (This could be called destructive learning and is not the best way to learn.)

- Capacitors are labeled in various ways, such as 0.01. This means that the unit is the µF. Sometimes the unit is marked 4.7 MFD. This is an old system that µF replaces. Some small caps are labeled 103. These types of caps have a value of 10 x 10^3 pF or 10,000 pF or 0.01 µF. Other markings are 104, 102, and 101. Use a similar method to identify the values. Learn to recognize these types of markings.

- In an RC series circuit, the charging current is maximum when the switch is closed. In one time constant (τ = RC), the voltage across the capacitor will increase to 63.2% of the voltage the capacitor is in parallel with. In each succeeding time constant, the voltage will increase to 63.2% of the remaining voltage difference. Assembled in a table, these voltages will be as follows (supply voltage = 100 V):

  At end of the 1st τ V_C = 63.2 V
  At end of the 2nd τ V_C = 86.5 V
  At end of the 3rd τ V_C = 95.0 V
  At end of the 4th τ V_C = 98.0 V
  At end of the 5th τ V_C = 100 V

  The capacitor is considered fully charged after 5 τ. To find the value of voltage with any other supply, just multiply the supply voltage by these percentages.

- A phase angle between the voltage across a capacitor and the current through it is always present. The current leads the voltage. To help you remember this relationship, use the acronym ICE for "I before **E** in a **C**apacitive circuit." Remember E is also a symbol for voltage. We will complete this phrase in the next chapter.

CHAPTER 10 QUIZ

Student Name ____

1. The measure of a capacitor's ability to store charge is called capacitance.
   a. true
   b. false

2. A capacitor blocks ac and passes dc.
   a. true
   b. false

3. If two capacitors are in series across a dc source, the largest capacitor has the largest voltage across it.
   a. true
   b. false

4. If the area of the plates of a capacitor is increased, the capacitance increases.
   a. true
   b. false

5. The time required for a capacitor to charge by 63.2% is called the time constant.
   a. true
   b. false

6. A capacitor has a charge of 2500 μC and a voltage across it of 25 V. The capacitance is
   a. 0.01 μF
   b. 0.1 μF
   c. 10 μF
   d. 100 μF

7. A 4.7 μF capacitor has a voltage across it of 50 V. What charge is stored in the capacitor?
   a. 235 μC
   b. 470 μC
   c. 23.5 μC
   d. 235 μC

8. The dc working voltage of a capacitor is 100 V. This means that the dielectric must be able to withstand
   a. 100 V dc
   b. 100 V_{peak}
   c. 200 V_{p-p}
   d. all of the above

9. Two equal value capacitors of 200 μF each are in parallel across 50 V. What is C_T and the voltage across each capacitor?
   a. 100 μF and 25 V
   b. 400 μF and 50 V
   c. 400 μF and 25 V
   d. 200 μF and 50 V

10. Three capacitors are in series. C_1 = 100 μF, C_2 = 100 μF, and C_3 = 50 μF. The source voltage is 75 V. What is the voltage across C_3?
   a. 18.75 V
   b. 50 V
   c. 37.5 V
   d. 100 V

11. A 0.001 μF capacitor is in series with a 10 kΩ resistor. What is the circuit's time constant?
   a. 10 μs
   b. 100 μs
   c. 0.1 s
   d. 1 s

12. A 0.047 μF capacitor is in series with a 1 MΩ resistor. How long will it take to completely charge the capacitor? The supply voltage is 50 V.
   a. 0.047 s
   b. 0.029 s
   c. 0.235 s
   d. 0.47 s

13. A 100 μF capacitor is charged to 25 V. You attempt to discharge the capacitor through a 22 kΩ resistor. How long will it take to completely discharge?
   a. 2.2 s
   b. 4.4 s
   c. 22 s
   d. 132 s

14. A 0.01 μF capacitor is in series with a 2.2 kΩ resistor. A voltage of 30 V is applied when a switch is closed. What will the voltage across the capacitor be after one time constant?
   a. 29.4 V
   b. 28.50 V
   c. 25.95 V
   d. 18.96 V

15. A 2.2 μF capacitor with a 1-kHz ac voltage applied to it will have ________X_C.
  a. infinite
  b. zero
  c. 72.4 Ω
  d. 0.013 Ω

16. A 159 pF capacitor has an X_C of 502 Ω. What is the operating frequency?
  a. 2 kHz
  b. 20 kHz
  c. 200 kHz
  d. 2000 kHz

17. An ohmmeter is used to test the resistance of a capacitor. The reading in both directions is 0 Ω. The capacitor is probably
  a. open.
  b. shorted.
  c. leaking.
  d. completely charged.

18. If the frequency applied to a capacitor is increased, the capacitive reactance will
  a. increase.
  b. decrease.
  c. remain the same.
  d. vary up and down.

19. A 47-μF capacitor is connected to a 5-V 400 Hz source. The current will be
  a. 590 mA
  b. 1.69 mA
  c. 94 mA
  d. 188 mA

20. A capacitor that will transfer an ac signal from one stage to another is called
  a. a bypass capacitor.
  b. a filter capacitor.
  c. a coupling capacitor.
  d. a transfer capacitor.

REVIEW OF KEY POINTS IN CHAPTER 11

INDUCTORS

INDUCTANCE AND INDUCTORS

- A length of wire wound in a coil is an inductor.
- A current flowing through the inductor forms a magnetic field with north and south poles.
- The symbol for inductance is L.
- The basic unit of inductance is the henry (H). In electronics we also use mH and μH.
- A coil of wire with current flowing through it has energy stored in the magnetic field.
- If the current through an inductor is changing, a voltage is induced. This property is called **inductance.**
- The physical characteristics of an inductor depend upon the following:
    - The material over which the coil is wound
    - The number of turns of wire in the coil
    - The size of the wire
- An inductor has some resistance as well as inductance because it is made of wire. The more turns of wire, the larger the resistance.
- Lenz's law says that when the current through a coil changes, the induced voltage has a polarity that opposes the change of current.

INDUCTOR TYPES

- The core material generally determines the type of inductor.
- There are air coil, iron core, and ferrite core inductors.
- Inductors can be made variable as well. Radio and TV tuners often use variable inductors.

INDUCTORS IN CIRCUITS

- Inductors connected in series combine similar to resistors in series. $L_T = L_1 + L_2 + L_3 + \ldots + L_n$
- The largest series inductor will have the greatest voltage across it.
- Inductors in parallel combine like resistors in parallel.
- The total inductance of inductors in parallel is always less than the smallest inductor.

INDUCTORS IN dc CIRCUITS

- If a dc current is flowing through an inductor, there is no induced voltage. The winding resistance voltage drop is present though.
- When an inductor is connected across a dc supply, the current increases in a nonlinear fashion.
- If a switch is used to connect the inductor to the source, the instant the switch is closed the current is zero. The induced voltage across the coil is maximum.
- After the switch is closed, the current increases until the magnetic field is completely built up.
- The time constant (τ) in an RL circuit is L/R_T. The formula is $\tau = L/R_T$.
- The time constant is the time for all voltages and currents to change to 63.2% of the maximum change. This is similar to capacitive circuits.
- When first energized, an inductor appears as an open circuit because the current is zero.

INDUCTORS IN ac CIRCUITS

- There is always a phase shift between the voltage across an inductor and the current through it.
- The voltage across the inductor <u>leads</u> the current by 90°.

- An inductor offers an opposition the flow of ac current. This is called **inductive reactance** (X_L). The unit of X_L is the ohm (Ω). The formula for X_L is $X_L = 2\pi fL$

- As the ac frequency is increased, the inductive reactance increases.

OHM'S LAW AND POWER

- Ohm's law is applied by using X_L as resistance is used in a dc circuit. $I_L = V_L/X_L$. The other forms follow similarly.

- True power is zero because most of the energy taken from the source to establish the magnetic field is returned to the source when the field collapses.

- Reactive power (P_r) is found by applying the power formulas. Substitute X_L for resistance:

$$P_r = V^2_{rms}/X_L$$

INDUCTOR USES

- Inductors are used in some power supply filters.

- At radio frequencies, an inductor is sometimes called a radio frequency choke (RFC). An RFC acts as an open to ac and a short to dc, because X_L is very high and the dc resistance is low.

- Inductors are used in tuned circuits with capacitors to provide frequency selection, as in a radio.

TECHNICIAN TIPS

- In an RL series circuit, the induced (reverse) voltage in the coil is maximum when the switch is first closed. Thus, current in the circuit is zero. In one time constant (τ = L/R), the current through the inductor will increase to 63.2% of the maximum circuit current. In each succeeding time constant, the current will increase by 63.2% of the available current maximum. The percentages are similar to those found in the table in the Technician Tips section on capacitors (Chapter 10). Remember, when first energized, the current increases, the voltage across the resistor in series increases, and the voltage across the inductance will decrease.

- The energy stored in a built-up magnetic field will continue to cause the current to flow in the same direction as the original current when the circuit is interrupted. The faster the circuit is opened, the greater the induced voltage. Automobile ignition systems use this inductive kick to build up the high voltage used in the spark plug. Television picture tubes also use this high-voltage energy to cause the electrons to move to the screen and produce the picture.

- The phase angle between the voltage across the inductor and the current through it is always present. The voltage leads the current. To help you remember this relationship, use the acronym ELI. Interpret this as in an inductive circuit (L), the voltage (E) leads the current (I). To use this acronym, remember that E is the other (less used) symbol for voltage.

- Recall the acronym ICE from Chapter 10. We can put the entire acronym phrase together for inductive and capacitive circuits. That is, ELI the ICE man. In an inductive circuit, the voltage leads the current and in a capacitive circuit the current leads the voltage. Use this acromym phrase or another, but remember these relationships.

CHAPTER 11 QUIZ

Student Name ____

1. The total inductance of series inductors is the sum of all the inductances.
   a. true
   b. false

2. The energy stored in an inductor's electrostatic field is produced by the current.
   a. true
   b. false

3. An inductor passes ac and opposes dc.
   a. true
   b. false

4. Inductive reactance increases when the frequency is increased.
   a. true
   b. false

5. In an inductive circuit, the current leads the voltage.
   a. true
   b. false

6. Two 2.5-mH inductors are in series with a 4.7-kΩ resistor. The source voltage is 100 V. What is the maximum current in this circuit?
   a. 21.3 mA
   b. 63.2 mA
   c. 1.1 mA
   d. 7.9 mA

7. An inductor has a dc current flowing through it. The magnetic field
   a. is changing constantly.
   b. is collapsing.
   c. is said to move from south to north.
   d. is said to move from north to south.

8. If a coil of wire is wound on an iron rod, the magnetic field
   a. is weaker than if a paper tube were used as the core.
   b. is weaker than if the core were air.
   c. is stronger than a coil wound on a paper tube.
   d. will collapse.

9. A frequency of 10 kHz is applied to a coil with an inductance of 150 mH. What is the inductive reactance?
   a. 1500 Ω
   b. 6280 Ω
   c. 8450 Ω
   d. 9420 Ω

10. In an inductive circuit, the ________leads the _________.
   a. voltage, power
   b. current, voltage
   c. voltage, current
   d. power, current

11. As frequency is increased, X_L
   a. increases
   d. decreases
   c. remains the same
   d. changes up and down

12. A 50-mH inductor has an X_L of 5000 Ω. What is the applied frequency?
   a. 159 Hz
   b. 1590 Hz
   c. 15,923 Hz
   d. 159,235 Hz

13. A 50-mH inductor is in series with a 5-kΩ resistor. What is the time constant?
   a. 10 μs
   b. 100 s
   c. 250 s
   d. 10 ms

14. How many time constants does it take to completely build up a magnetic field around an inductor?
   a. one
   b. two
   c. four
   d. five

15. A series inductor with an inductance of 10 mH and a winding resistance of 50 Ω is applied to a 500-Hz source. What is the inductive reactance?
   a. 0.032 Ω
   b. 31.4 Ω
   c. 0.5 Ω
   d. 31.4 kΩ

16. A 40-mH inductor is in parallel with a 24-mH inductor. The total inductance is
a. 64 mH
b. 32 mH
c. 15.39 mH
d. 153.9 mH

17. You think that an inductor is faulty. You measure the resistance at 0 Ω. The dc voltage across the coil measures zero. The probable fault, if any, is
a. the coil is shorted.
b. the coil is open.
c. the coil is normal.
d. the coil will work on ac.

18. An inductor is placed in an ac circuit with a voltage of 20 V. The current is 250 mA. What is the inductive reactance?
a. 0.0125 Ω
b. 160 Ω
c. 80 Ω
d. cannot compute, no frequency given

19. If 50 V at a frequency of 5 kHz were measured across an inductor with an inductance of 500 mH, what would be the current?
a. 6.36 mA
b. 3.18 mA
c. 1.59 mA
d. 0.08 mA

20. A coil of wire is carrying a dc current of 50 mA. The X_C of the coil at 60 Hz is 400 Ω. The voltage across the coil is 25 V. What is the resistance of the coil?
a. 500 Ω
b. 400 Ω
c. 16 Ω
d. 20 Ω

REVIEW OF KEY POINTS IN CHAPTER 12

TRANSFORMERS

TRANSFORMER OPERATION

- Transformers generally have two windings, a primary winding and a secondary winding. These windings are close to each other so that a magnetic field around the primary will affect the coil of the secondary. This is called **mutual inductance**.

- A voltage applied to the primary winding causes a magnetic field to build up. This increase in the magnetic field induces a corresponding voltage in the secondary winding.

- The coils of a transformer are wound around a core. This core can be air, iron, or other magnetic material.

- If an ac voltage is applied to the primary winding, an ac voltage is induced in the secondary winding.

- Sometimes transformer windings are wound one around the other for maximum coupling between them.

- Transformers require a changing voltage to operate; therefore, they effectively block dc from primary to secondary.

TRANSFORMER TYPES

- **Turns ratio** ($n = N_s/N_p$) is the ratio of the secondary turns to the primary turns.

- A step-up transformer steps up or increases the secondary voltage to a larger value than the primary.

- In a step-down transformer, the secondary voltage is lower than the primary voltage.

- The formula to find secondary voltage is $V_s = (N_s/N_p)V_p$ for either a step-up or a step-down transformer.

- An ideal transformer has no power loss. The power delivered to the primary is equal to the power delivered to the load.

- The current in the secondary when a load is connected is found by $I_s = (N_p/N_s)I_p$.

- A load on the secondary is reflected back to the primary. This load resistance the primary will see is found by $R_{ref} = (1/n)^2 R_L$.

MAXIMUM POWER TRANSFER

- Maximum power transfer from a source to a load occurs when the internal resistance of a source equals the resistance of a load.

- Transformers are often used to match the impedance of a source to the impedance of a load.

TRANSFORMER CHARACTERISTICS

- The windings of a transformer are made of wire that has resistance. One type of loss in a transformer is the power loss due to winding resistance when current flows in the coils.

- **Hysteresis** loss is caused by the rapid reversal of the magnetic field heating the iron coil.

- The loss due to the current flowing in an iron core is called **eddy current** loss.

- Lamimating the transformer core reduces eddy current losses.

- Power transformers are efficient devices. Efficiencies of 95% are common.

- Some types of transformers have multiple windings. Also, some have taps or connections to the center or to other parts of a winding. A center-tapped secondary is typical.

- Transformer windings may open or turns may short together.

TECHNICIAN TIPS

- Transformers transform the voltage directly as the turns ratio. This means that if the turns ratio is greater than one, the transformer is a step-up type. The reverse is also true. Transformers transform the current inversely as the turns ratio. Transformers transform the impedance directly as the square of the turns ratio. A step-down transformer steps the voltage down, steps the current up, and steps the impedance down by the turns ratio squared.

- The principal of maximum power transfer is useful. For example, a TV antenna may have an impedance of 300 ohms. To match this antenna to a transmission line with an impedance of 75 ohms, a matching transformer is used. This will ensure that the maximum power on the antenna will be transferred to the transmission line. Connecting speakers to an amplifier often involves the use of a matching transformer.

- Transformers are relatively trouble free. Windings can be checked with an ohmmeter for an open condition, that is, infinite resistance. A shorted winding can be checked with a ohmmeter as well; however, power transformer primary windings usually have a very low resistance. Be on the watch for low resistances may not be an indication of trouble.

CHAPTER 12 QUIZ

Student Name ____

1. The number of turns in the primary and secondary determines the turns ratio.
   a. true
   b. false

2. Maximum power is moved from the secondary to the primary when the source resistance is equal to the load resistance.
   a. true
   b. false

3. A transformer with a turns ratio of 0.5 is a step-up transformer.
   a. true
   b. false

4. The core materials of transformers are often laminated iron or air.
   a. true
   b. false

5. Transformers are efficient devices.
   a. true
   b. false

6. A step-down transformer will decrease__________ and increase __________.
   a. resistance, power
   b. current, voltage
   c. voltage, current
   d. power, current

7. The loss in a transformer due to the changing magnetic field is called
   a. eddy current loss.
   b. hysteresis loss.
   c. I^2R loss.
   d. flux leakage loss.

8. A step-up transformer will increase__________ and decrease__________.
   a. voltage, impedance
   b. voltage, power
   c. current, impedance
   d. power, current

9. The loss in a transformer due to currents flowing in the core is called
   a. hysteresis loss.
   b. winding loss.
   c. flux leakage loss.
   d. eddy current loss.

10. To transfer the most power from the source to the load,
   a. the source resistance must be larger than the load resistance.
   b. the load resistance must equal the power loss.
   c. the source resistance must equal the load resistance.
   d. the power in the primary and secondary must be equal.

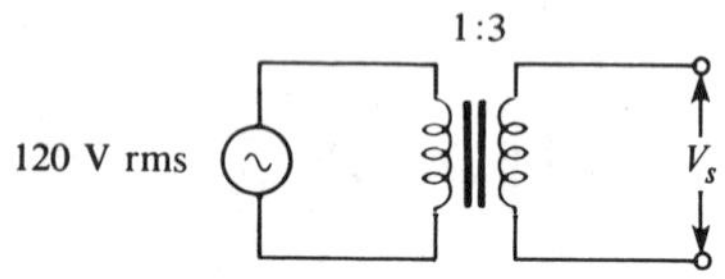

FIGURE 12-1

11. See Figure 12-1. There are five times as many turns in the secondary as the primary. What is the secondary voltage, V_S?
   a. 24 V
   b. 240 V
   c. 560 V
   d. 600 V

12. See Figure 12-1. If the ratio of primary to secondary turns is 4.5:1, what is the output voltage, V_S?
   a. 540 V
   b. 26.67 V
   c. 5.92 V
   d. 4.72 V

13. See Figure 12-1. If the primary to secondary turns ratio is 4:1, and a load resistor of 50 Ð is in the secondary, what is the secondary current?
   a. 1.66 A
   b. 600 mA
   c. 9.6 A
   d. 4.8 A

14. See Figure 12-1. The primary to secondary turns ratio is 4:1 and I_S = 40 mA. What is the primary current?
   a. 160 mA
   b. 40 mA
   c. 4 mA
   d. cannot compute

15. See Figure 12-1. The primary to secondary turns ratio is 4:1 and I_S = 40 mA. What is the reflected resistance seen by the primary?
a. 4 kΩ
b. 8 kΩ
c. 12 kΩ
d. 16 kΩ

16. What ratio would transform 100 V into 40 V?
a. 40:100
b. 4:1
c. 400:1000
d. 2.5:1

17. The primary to secondary turns ratio is 60:5 and the primary voltage and current is 120 V and 75 mA. What is the primary power?
a. 0.75 W
b. 1.25 W
c. 9 W
d. 9.6 W

18. A transformer measures full voltage across the primary terminals but there is no voltage delivered to the load. The trouble might be
a. a short across the secondary.
b. an open primary.
c. a shorted primary.
d. an open transformer core.

19. You desire to match a 300-Ω load to a 75-Ω source. What would be the turns ratio of the transformer?
a. 1:2
b. 2:1
c. 1:4
d. 4:1

20. You have a need to isolate two circuits with no change of voltage. You would use a/an_____________transformer with a turns ratio of ________.
a. step-up, 2:1
b. step-down, 1:1
c. step-up, 1:1
d. isolation, 1:1

REVIEW OF KEY POINTS IN CHAPTER 13

FREQUENCY RESPONSE OF RC CIRCUITS

ac RESPONSE OF RC SERIES CIRCUITS

- Frequency does not change when ac is applied to a circuit with resistors and capacitors.
- The total opposition to the flow of ac current is called **impedance** and the unit is ohms.
- The current through a resistor in an ac circuit is in phase with the voltage.
- The current through a capacitor in an ac circuit leads the voltage by 90°.
- In an ac circuit with R and C in series, the phase angle is between 0° and 90°.
- Phasors are used to solve the circuit conditions in an RC circuit.
- The impedance is found by adding the directional vectors or phasors graphically.
- The formula for impedance is $Z = \sqrt{R^2 + X_C^2}$.
- The phase angle is found by $\Theta = \arctan(X_C/R)$.
- Ohm's law can be applied to an RC circuit by substituting Z for R in all the formulas: $V = IZ$, $I = V/Z$, and $Z = V/I$.
- The voltages in a series RC circuit can be found using the formula $V_S = \sqrt{V_R^2 + V_C^2}$.
- The phase angle is also found by $\Theta = \arctan(V_C/V_R)$.
- When the frequency increases, X_C decreases, Z decreases, and the phase angle (Θ) decreases.

ac RESPONSE OF RC PARALLEL CIRCUITS

- In a parallel RC circuit, the impedance is found by the product over sum formula, $Z = \dfrac{RX_C}{\sqrt{R^2 + X_C^2}}$.

- In a parallel RC circuit, the currents are added using this formula, $I_T = \sqrt{I_R^2 + I_C^2}$.
- The phase angle is found by $\Theta = \arctan(I_C/I_R)$.

POWER IN RC CIRCUITS

- There is power dissipated in an RC circuit. Some energy is stored in the capacitor and returned to the source. The resistor dissipates power.
- The formula for the power dissipated by the resistor is called **true power** (P_{true}). $P_{true} = I_R^2 R$ and the unit is watts.
- The reactive power is found by $P_r = I_C^2 X_C$ and the unit is the volt-ampere reactive (VAR).
- The resultant power is called **apparent power**, P_a, and is found by $P_a = I_T^2 Z$. The unit is the volt-ampere (VA).
- The power factor (PF) is the cos of Θ, the phase angle, and is stated PF = cos Θ. There are no units.

LEAD-LAG RC CIRCUITS

- In an RC lag circuit, the voltage output is taken across the capacitor. The output voltage lags the input voltage.
- In an RC lead circuit, the output is taken across the resistor. The output voltage leads the input voltage.

RC FILTERS

- A **filter** is a circuit that passes certain frequencies while blocking other frequencies.
- An RC **low-pass filter** is a series RC circuit with the output taken across the capacitor.
- A low-pass filter passes lower frequencies and blocks higher frequencies.
- An RC **high-pass filter** is a series RC circuit with the output taken across the resistor.

- A high-pass filter passes higher frequencies and blocks lower frequencies.

- The **cutoff frequency** is the frequency where the output from the filter has a value of 70.7% of the maximum output voltage.

- The formula for the cutoff frequency for either a high-pass or low-pass filter is $f_c = 1/2\pi RC$. The unit is Hz.

- Filter problems can be caused by open, shorted, or leaky capacitors. A resistor can also open.

TECHNICIAN TIPS

- Impedance is the total opposition to current in an ac circuit. Since in an RC circuit the voltage across the resistor and across the capacitor are 90° out of phase with each other (remember ICE), the voltages are added according to Kirchhoff's law. However, remember that they are added graphically using phasor diagrams. The Pythagorean theorem gives us the correct formula to use. The voltages across the components are added using the similar method. Kirchhoff's law still works but add voltages or oppositions by using the triangles.

- A parallel RC circuit can be analyzed by using conductance, susceptance, and admittance. An alternate method would be to solve for the currents in each branch. Use Ohm's law for this. Then add the currents by using the triangle. $I_T = \sqrt{I_C^2 + I_R^2}$. The total impedance can then be found by $Z_T = V_T/I_T$.

- Filters using RC networks are common in electronics. The components, though, can fail and circuits will not work correctly. In a low-pass filter, the output is taken across the capacitor. If the capacitor opens, there will be no filtering action. If the resistor opens, no output signal will be observed. An open resistor in a high-pass filter will reduce the cutoff frequency. An open capacitor will give no output signal.

- A low-pass filter is used in filter circuits for power supplies. An open electrolytic capacitor is a common problem. Electrolytic capacitors also become leaky. A leaky capacitor will produce some filtering action but the output voltage will be reduced. A shorted capacitor will produce zero output.

CHAPTER 13 QUIZ

Student Name ______________________________

1. When a sine wave is applied to an RC circuit, the current and all the voltage drops are also sine waves.
   a. true
   b. false

2. The current in an RC series circuit always lags the source voltage.
   a. true
   b. false

3. The phasor combination of true power and reactive power is called apparent power.
   a. true
   b. false

4. A filter blocks certain frequencies and passes others.
   a. true
   b. false

5. The phase angle of a series RC circuit varies directly with frequency.
   a. true
   b. false

6. See Figure 13-1. Calculate for the total impedance.
   a. 418 Ω
   b. 520 Ω
   c. 280 Ω
   d. 120 Ω

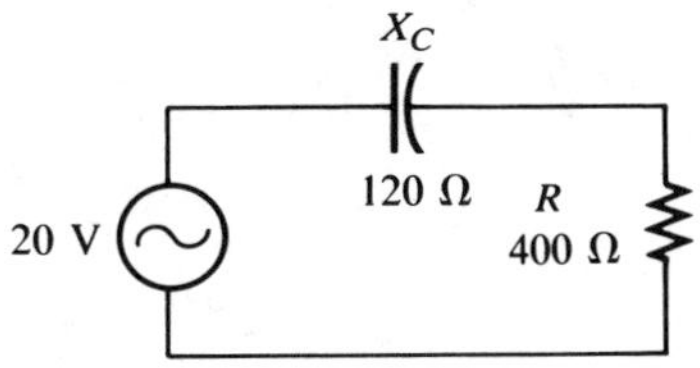

FIGURE 13-1

7. See Figure 13-1. Calculate the phase angle.
   a. 73.3°
   b. 17.5°
   c. 16.7°
   d. 72.5°

8. See Figure 13-1. Calculate the voltage drop across the capacitor.
   a. 19.14 V
   b. 16.7 V
   c. 20 V
   d. 5.75 V

9. See Figure 13-1. Calculate the true power.
   a. 275 mW
   b. 916 mW
   c. 956 mW
   d. 1002 mW

10. See Figure 13-1. Calculate the apparent power.
   a. 0.874 VA
   b. 0.916 VA
   c. 0.957 VA
   d. 0.989 VA

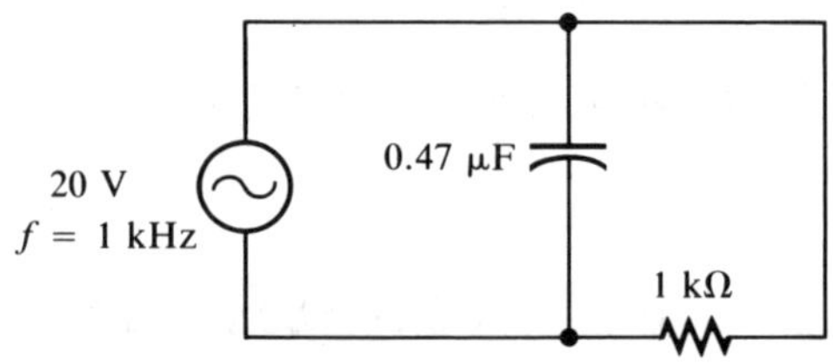

FIGURE 13-2

11. See Figure 13-2. Find the current through the capacitor.
   a. 20 mA
   b. 62 mA
   c. 321 mA
   d. 59 mA

12. See Figure 13-2. Find the total impedance.
   a. 1000 Ω
   b. 880 Ω
   c. 321 Ω
   d. 62 Ω

13. See Figure 13-2. Find the phase angle.
   a. 18.7°
   b. 71.3°
   c. 14.7°
   d. 3.2°

14. See Figure 13-2. Find the apparent power.
   a. 1.18 VA
   b. 0.4 VA
   c. 1.246 VA
   d. 0.95 VA

15. See Figure 13-2. What is the power factor?
   a. 0.947
   b. 0.321
   c. 0.338
   d. 2.95

16. See Figure 13-1. If the frequency is increased, the phase angle will__________and the impedance will__________.
   a. decrease, increase
   b. increase, decrease
   c. decrease, decrease
   d. increase, increase

17. See Figure 13-2. If the frequency is decreased, the total current will__________and the total impedance will__________.
   a. decrease, increase
   b. increase, decrease
   c. decrease, decrease
   d. increase, increase

18. See Figure 13-1. If the output were across the resistor, the circuit would be known as a
   a. low-pass filter.
   b. high-pass filter.
   c. band-pass filter.
   d. band-reject filter.

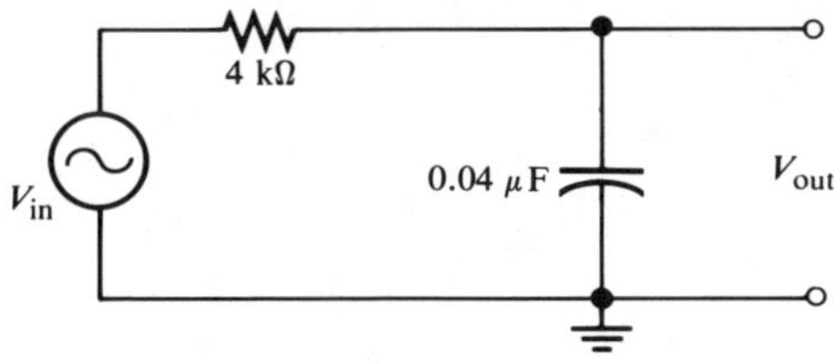

FIGURE 13-3

19. See Figure 13-3. The cutoff frequency is
   a. 6250 Hz
   b. 99 Hz
   c. 480 Hz
   d. 995 Hz

20. See Figure 13-3. If the input voltage were 17 V, what would the voltage be across the capacitor at the cutoff frequency?
    a. 0 V
    b. 8 V
    c. 12 V
    d. 17 V

REVIEW OF KEY POINTS IN CHAPTER 14

FREQUENCY RESPONSE OF RL CIRCUITS

ac RESPONSE OF RL SERIES CIRCUITS

- Frequency does not change when ac is applied to a circuit with resistors and inductors.
- The current through an inductor in an ac circuit lags the driving voltage by 90°.
- The impedance is found by adding the phasors.
- The formula for impedance is $Z = \sqrt{R^2 + X_L^2}$.
- The phase angle is found by $\Theta = \arctan(X_L/R)$.
- Ohm's law can be applied to an RL circuit by substituting Z for R in the formulas. $V = IZ$, $I = V/Z$, and $Z = V/I$.
- The voltages can be found in a series RL circuit by a form of $V_S = \sqrt{V_R^2 + V_L^2}$
- When the frequency increases, X_L increases, Z increases, and the phase angle (Θ) increases.

ac RESPONSE OF RL PARALLEL CIRCUITS

- In a parallel RL circuit, the impedance is found by the product over sum formula, $Z = \dfrac{RX_L}{\sqrt{R^2 + X_L^2}}$
- In a parallel RL circuit, the currents are added using this formula, $I_T = \sqrt{I_R^2 + I_L^2}$.
- The phase angle between the resistor current and the total current is found by $\Theta = \arctan(I_L/I_R)$.

POWER IN RL CIRCUITS

- There is power dissipated in an RL circuit. The energy stored in the magnetic field around the inductor is returned to the source. This is reactive power. The resistor dissipates true power.

- The formula for the power dissipated by the resistor is $P_{true} = I_R^2R$ and the unit is the watt.
- The reactive power is found by $P_r = I_L^2X_L$ and the unit is the volt-ampere reactive (VAR).
- The resultant power is called apparent power, P_a, and is found by $P_a = I_T^2Z$. The unit is the volt-ampere (VA).
- The power factor (PF) is the cosine of the phase angle, and the formula is PF = cos Θ.

LEAD-LAG RL CIRCUITS

- In an RL lag network, the output is taken across the resistor. The output voltage lags the input voltage.
- In an RL lead circuit, the output voltage is taken across the inductor. The output voltage leads the input voltage.

RL FILTERS

- An RL low-pass filter is a series RL circuit with the output taken across the resistor.
- An RL high-pass filter is a series RL circuit with the output taken across the inductor.
- The formula for the cutoff frequency of either a high-pass or low-pass RL filter is $f_c = \frac{1}{2\pi(L/R)}$

TECHNICIAN TIPS

- Impedance is the total opposition to the current in an RC circuit. This is the same in an RL as well as in an RC circuit. In a series RL circuit, the voltages across the resistor and the inductor are 90° out of phases. Remember ELI the ICE man. The voltage drops across the resistor and the inductor are added as in Kirchhoff's law, but they are added according to the Pythagorean theorem. Use phasor diagrams to add these voltages.

- As in RC circuits, a parallel RL circuit can be analyzed by using conductance, susceptance, and admittance. The alternate method we used in RC parallel circuits can also be used in RL circuits. Determine the currents in each branch and add them according to the formula $I_T = \sqrt{I_R^2 + I_L^2}$. Find impedance by $Z = V/I_T$.

- If the inductor opens in a low-pass filter, the output will be zero. If the resistor opens, the cutoff frequency will increase. If the inductor should short in a low-pass filter, there will be no filtering action at all.

- In an RL high-pass filter, an open inductor will cause a loss of filter action. An open resistor will cause the output signal to be zero.

- As you can see, the characteristics of the RL filter are opposite to those of the RC filter. Learn the RC filter and you need only remember RL characteristics are opposite.

CHAPTER 14 QUIZ

Student Name ____

1. Total current in an RL circuit always leads the source voltage.
   a. true
   b. false

2. A low-pass filter passes low frequencies and blocks other frequencies.
   a. true
   b. false

3. The impedance of an RL circuit varies directly with frequency.
   a. true
   b. false

4. In a filter circuit using RL components, an increase in the value of R will increase the cutoff frequency.
   a. true
   b. false

5. The impedance of a parallel RL circuit is found by adding X_L to R.
   a. true
   b. false

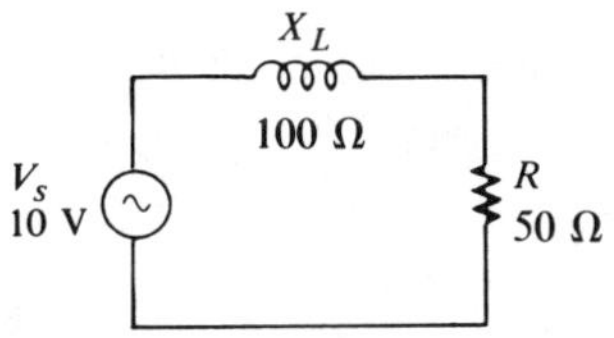

FIGURE 14-1

6. See Figure 14-1. Find the impedance.
   a. 104 Ω
   b. 112 Ω
   c. 1120 Ω
   d. 1040 Ω

7. See Figure 14-1. Find the phase angle.
   a. 26.6°
   b. 0.034°
   c. 63.4°
   d. 45°

8. See Figure 14-1. Find the voltage across the inductor.
   a. 0.4 V
   b. 0.894 V
   c. 4.47 V
   d. 8.94 V

9. See Figure 14-1. Find the true power.
   a. 400 mW
   b. 0.894 W
   c. 0.8 W
   d. 112 mW

10. See Figure 14-1. Find the apparent power.
   a. 0.4 VA
   b. 0.8 VA
   c. 8.94 VA
   d. 0.894 VA

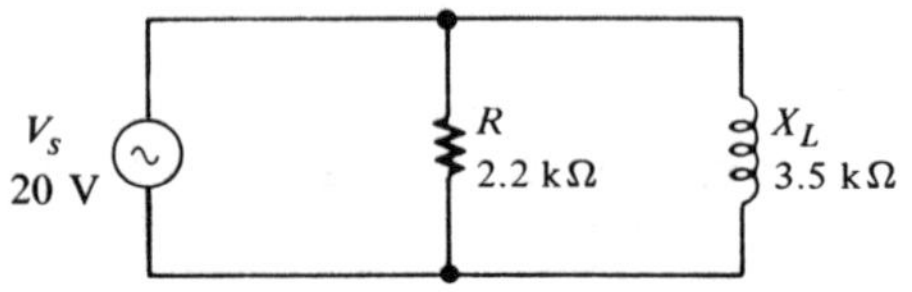

FIGURE 14-2

11. See Figure 14-2. Find the current through the inductor.
   a. 5.71 mA
   b. 0.182 mA
   c. 9.09 mA
   d. 2.15 mA

12. See Figure 14-2. Find the total impedance.
   a. 10.74 kΩ
   b. 9.09 kΩ
   c. 5.71 kΩ
   d. 1.86 kΩ

13. See Figure 14-2. Find the phase angle.
   a. 32.15°
   b. 57.85°
   c. 45°
   d. 53.2°

14. See Figure 14-2. Find the apparent power.
   a. 0.182 VA
   b. 0.532 VA
   c. 1.86 VA
   d. 0.215 VA

15. See Figure 14-2. Find the power factor.
   a. 0.707
   b. 0.846
   c. 0.532
   d. 0.599

16. See Figure 14-1. If the frequency is increased, the phase angle will__________ and the impedance will__________.
   a. decrease, increase
   b. increase, decrease
   c. decrease, decrease
   d. increase, increase

17. See Figure 14-2. If the frequency is decreased, the total current will__________and the total impedance will__________.
   a. decrease, increase
   b. increase, decrease
   c. decrease, decrease
   d. increase, increase

18. See Figure 14-1. If the output were across the resistor, the circuit would be known as a
   a. low-pass filter.
   b. high-pass filter.
   c. band-pass filter.
   d. band-reject filter.

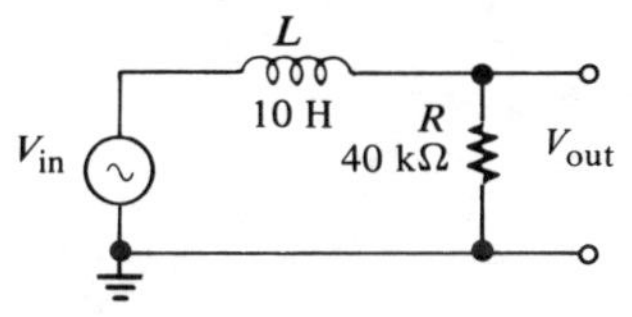

FIGURE 14-3

19. See Figure 14-3. Find the cutoff frequency.
   a. 2.5 MHz
   b. 637 Hz
   c. 1.2 MHz
   d. 408 Hz

20. See Figure 14-3. If the input voltage were 21 V, find the output voltage at the cutoff frequency.
   a. 0 V
   b. 6.15 V
   c. 14.85 V
   d. 21 V

REVIEW OF KEY POINTS IN CHAPTER 15

RESONANT CIRCUITS

SERIES RLC CIRCUITS

- A series RLC circuit contains resistance, X_L, and X_C.
- The effects of X_L and X_C are 180° out of phase and so subtract from each other.
- The formula for impedance in a series RLC circuit is as follows: $Z = \sqrt{R^2 + (X_L - X_C)^2}$. Be sure to use the actual difference between the reactances as a positive number.
- The phase angle is $\Theta = \arctan(X_T/R)$, where $X_T = X_L \pm X_C$.
- The voltages across the inductor and capacitor are always 180° out of phase with each other, and each is 90° out of phase with the resistor, if any, in the circuit.

SERIES RESONANCE

- For every series RLC circuit there is a frequency when $X_L = X_C$. This frequency is the resonant frequency, f_r.
- At the resonant frequency, the circuit is said to be a resonant circuit.
- At resonance, the impedance equals the resistance. $Z_r = R$.
- The formula for the resonant frequency is $f_r = \dfrac{1}{2\pi\sqrt{LC}}$
- At frequencies below the resonant frequency, the circuit is capacitive.
- At frequencies above the resonant frequency, the circuit is inductive.
- The circuit current is maximum at resonance and decreases both above and below resonance.
- The total impedance is minimum at resonance and increases both above and below resonance.
- The phase angle of a series resonant circuit is 0°.

SERIES RESONANT FILTERS

- A series resonant circuit is often used as a band-pass filter.
- A band-pass filter passes a band of frequencies but blocks other frequencies above and below the pass band.
- Bandwidth, BW, is the band of frequencies between the upper and lower cutoff frequencies.
- The cutoff frequencies above and below resonance are at the point where the output of the circuit is 0.707 I or 0.707 V_{out}.
- The cutoff frequencies are f_1 (the lower cutoff frequency) and f_2 (the upper cutoff frequency). Other names are -3 dB frequencies, band frequencies, and half-power frequencies.
- The -3 dB term means that the response at the cutoff frequencies is down 3 decibels.
- The decibel formula for gain or loss can be expressed in voltage or power terms: $dB = 20 \log(V_{out}/V_{in})$ and $dB = 10 \log(P_{out}/P_{in})$. These formulas are true as long as $Z_{in} = Z_{out}$.
- The quality factor of a resonant circuit is $Q = X_L/R$.
- The higher the value of Q, the narrower the bandwidth. $BW = f_r/Q$.
- A band-stop or band-reject filter will reject frequencies within the pass-band and pass all others.
- A series resonant circuit is most often used as a band-stop filter.

PARALLEL RLC CIRCUITS

- The impedance of a parallel RLC circuit can be found using susceptance and admittance.

- The total current of a parallel RLC circuit is found by using Ohm's law, and summing the currents using $I_T = \sqrt{IR^2 + (I_L - I_C)^2}$
- The phase angle is found by $\Theta = \arctan(I_{CL}/I_T)$, where $I_{CL} = I_C \pm I_L$.

PARALLEL RESONANCE

- If the Q of the circuit is greater than about 10, then resonance in a parallel circuit occurs when $X_L = X_C$.
- The resonant frequency is found by $f_r = 1/2\pi\sqrt{LC}$.
- The currents in the inductor and capacitor are 180° out of phase with each other.
- The energy circulates between the inductor and the capacitor so a parallel resonant circuit is commonly called a tank circuit.
- If the Q of the circuit is low, less than about 10, the actual f_r varies from the ideal formula given above.
- At resonance the impedance of the circuit is maximum.
- At resonance the total current is minimum.
- An external load to a tank circuit will affect the overall Q of the circuit. This will affect the BW.
- At frequencies below resonance, the circuit is inductive.
- At frequencies above resonance, the circuit is capacitive in nature.

PARALLEL RESONANT FILTERS

- A parallel resonant circuit are most frequently used as a band-pass filter.
- The cutoff frequencies are f_1, the lower cutoff, and f_2, the upper cutoff.
- The bandwidth can be found by $BW = f_r/Q$ and also $BW = f_2 - f_1$.

- A band-stop filter can consist of a parallel resonant circuit in series with the signal path.

- Parallel resonant circuits, rather than series resonant circuits, are found in almost all types of communications equipment, such as amplifiers, transmitters, and TV receivers.

TECHNICIAN TIPS

- Every RLC circuit has a resonant frequency. These circuits may not always be operating at resonance. In communications equipment, parallel resonant circuits are used more than series resonant circuits because the total current is much less with a tank circuit. This means that the other circuits used to supply the currents at resonance can be much smaller in their current handling ability.

- The selectivity of a resonant circuit is controlled by Q. Selectivity is the circuit's ability to select only certain signals. The higher the Q, the narrower the bandwidth. In a series resonant circuit, a narrow bandwidth also produces a higher output voltage across the inductor or capacitor. The output from a resonant circuit is often transformer coupled to another circuit. The primary of the transformer acts as the inductor in the tank circuit. In this case, the secondary of the transformer also acts as additional inductance in the tank circuit and this will affect the resonant frequency.

- In a tank circuit (parallel resonant) with a Q greater than 10, $Q = I_{tank}/I_{line}$. I_{line} is the total current supplied to the circuit. Also if $Q \geq 10$, $Z_p = QX_L$. You can see that Q really ties the parallel circuit values together. If $Q < 10$, then these relationships are not true.

- In a resonant circuit where $Q \geq 10$, the resonant frequency is in the center of the pass band. From this you can determine the cutoff frequencies by $f_2 = f_r + BW/2$ and $f_1 = f_r - BW/2$. These can be handy formulas for your use.

CHAPTER 15 QUIZ

Student Name ______________________________

1. The total reactance of a series RLC circuit at resonance is zero.
   a. true
   b. false

2. At resonance, a series RLC circuit is capacitive.
   a. true
   b. false

3. If an RLC circuit is resonant, usually $X_L = X_C$.
   a. true
   b. false

4. The bandwidth of a resonant circuit varies directly with Q: as Q increases, the bandwidth increases.
   a. true
   b. false

5. A parallel resonant circuit has maximum impedance and minimum line current.
   a. true
   b. false

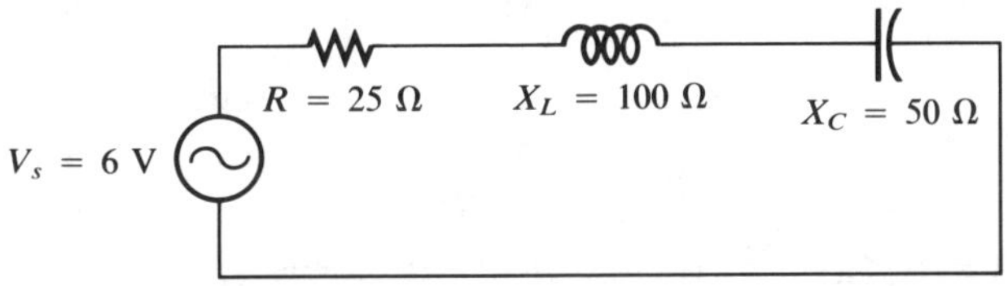

FIGURE 15-1

6. See Figure 15-1. Find the impedance of this circuit.
   a. 50 Ω
   b. 75 Ω
   c. 56 Ω
   d. 25 Ω

7. See Figure 15-1. If the frequency of the source voltage is decreased a little, the impedance will _________ and the phase angle will _________.
   a. increase, increase
   b. decrease, decrease
   c. increase, decrease
   d. decrease, increase

8. See Figure 15-1. Find the current.
   a. 107 mA
   b. 240 mA
   c. 120 mA
   d. 60 mA

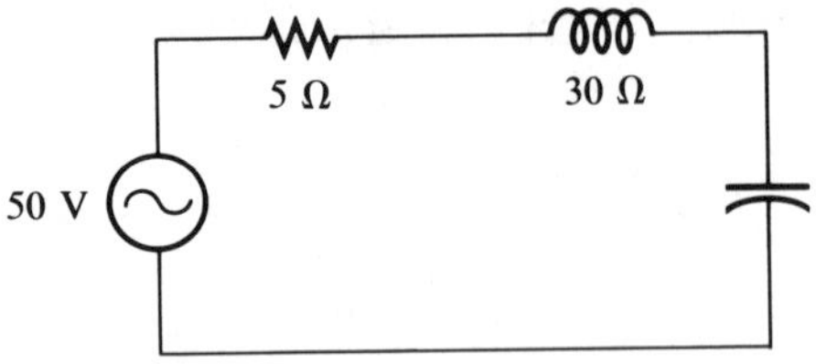

FIGURE 15-2

9. See Figure 15-2. At resonance the current will be
   a. 10 A
   b. 10 mA
   c. 1.66 A
   d. 1.66 mA

10. See Figure 15-2. The voltage across the resistor at resonance is
   a. 49.8 V
   b. 49.8 mV
   c. 50 mV
   d. 50 V

11. See Figure 15-2. At resonance, the voltage across the capacitor is
   a. 300 mV
   b. 300 V
   c. 30 V
   d. 3 V

12. In a resonant parallel RLC circuit, the impedance is__________ and the total current is __________.
   a. maximum, maximum
   b. minimum, minimum
   c. maximum, minimum
   d. minimum, maximum

13. A resonant circuit with a high Q means that it
   a. has a narrow pass band.
   b. tunes broadly.
   c. has a small voltage across the capacitor.
   d. has a wide pass band.

14. The resonant frequency of a tank circuit with L = 150 μH and with C = 300 pF is
a. 1.65 MHz
b. 751 kHz
c. 347 kHz
d. 6.05 MHz

15. What is the bandwidth of a circuit resonant at 500 kHz, if X_C = 2.5 kΩ and the coil resistance is 25 Ω?
a. 100 Hz
b. 1000 Hz
c. 2.5 kHz
d. 5 kHz

16. A circuit is resonant at 1 MHz. Q = 50. f_1 = __________ and f_2 = __________.
a. 0.98 MHz, 1.01 MHz
b. 0.99 MHz, 1.02 MHz
c. 0.99 MHz, 1.01 MHz
d. 0.98 MHZ, 1.02 MHz

17. The impedance of a parallel resonant circuit is 50 kΩ. The impedance of the circuit at the lower cutoff frequency is
a. 385 kΩ
b. 35.35 kΩ
c. 35.35 kHz
d. cannot compute, not enough data

18. The input voltage to a series resonant circuit is 120 mV. The output voltage across the inductor is 12.7 V. What is the voltage ratio of V_o to V_{in} expressed in decibels?
a. 105.8 dB
b. 20.2 dB
c. 40.4 dB
d. -19.5 dB

19. A resonant circuit is delivering 50 W of power. The power at the upper cutoff frequency is
a. 25 W
b. 35.35 W
c. 50 W
d. 70.7 W

20. A parallel resonant circuit has an X_C of 502 Ω. The source voltage is 25 V at a frequency of 14.9 MHz. What is the tank current? Q = 55.
a. 270 mA
b. 49.8 mA
c. 9.12 mA
d. 20.08 mA

REVIEW OF KEY POINTS IN CHAPTER 16

PULSE RESPONSE OF RC AND RL CIRCUITS

RC INTEGRATORS

- An RC integrator is a basic low-pass filter with a pulse applied to it.
- A pulse applied to the integrator circuit will charge the capacitor. When the pulse voltage is removed, the capacitor discharges.
- The output of an RC integrator is the capacitor voltage.
- If the input pulse width (t_W) is equal or greater that five time constants ($t_W \geq 5\tau$), the capacitor will completely charge to the supply voltage.
- If $t_W < 5\tau$, then the capacitor will not have time to completely charge. The maximum V_C will depend upon the relationship of the RC time constant to the pulse width.
- As the time constant gets longer, the maximum capacitor voltage gets smaller.
- When an RC integrator has a repetitive pulse applied to it, the average output voltage across the capacitor depends again upon the relationship of the RC time constant to the period of the incoming square wave pulses.
- If the time constant of the integrator is increased, the average output voltage will increase. This will approach dc if the time constant is increased to a large value.

RC DIFFERENTIATORS

- An RC differentiator is a basic high-pass filter with a pulse or square wave applied to it.
- In the RC differentiator, the output voltage is taken across the resistor.

- Again, we must consider the relationship of the pulse width to the time constant. If $t_w \geq 5\tau$, then the capacitor has time to fully charge. The output voltage will be the difference between the input voltage and the voltage across the capacitor. This voltage is maximum when the pulse is applied and decreases to zero.

- If $t_w < 5\tau$, the capacitor will not completely charge and the output voltage across the resistor will not decrease to zero.

- If the capacitor is fully charged and the pulse voltage is removed, the capacitor will discharge through the source and the voltage drop across the resistor will be maximum in the reverse direction. This will produce a negative spike of voltage across the output.

- A series of square wave pulses applied to an RC differentiator with a very short time constant will produce a series of positive and negative spikes.

- If the time constant is increased, the output voltage will approach the shape of the input voltage.

RL INTEGRATORS

- An RL integrator is a basic RL low-pass filter. The output is taken across the resistor.

- The output is exactly the same as the RC integrator.

RL DIFFERENTIATORS

- An RL differentiator is a basic RL high-pass filter. The output is taken across the inductor.

- The output is exactly the same as the RC differentiator.

TECHNICIAN TIPS

- Kirchhoff's law applies to all paths at all times. In an RC integrator, the voltage across the capacitor increases as the capacitor takes on a charge. At the same time, the circuit current and the voltage across the resistor is decreasing. These two voltages must add to the total source voltage. When the capacitor is discharging, the current is flowing in the opposite direction so the voltage that appears across the resistor is a negative spike. The width of this spike is, of course, dependent upon circuit values and the frequency of the square wave signal.

- RC integrators are used extensively in industrial control circuits to measure such things as the amount of exposure light in a photoprocessing machine. This will automatically compensate for light or dense negatives. Many other uses for these wave shaping circuits exist.

CHAPTER 16 QUIZ

Student Name ____

1. In an RC integrating circuit, the output is taken across the resistor.
   a. true
   b. false

2. In an integrator, when the pulse width of the input is much greater than 5τ, the output approaches the shape of the input.
   a. true
   b. false

3. In an RL integrating circuit, the output is taken across the resistor.
   a. true
   b. false

4. It takes a capacitor one time constant to completely charge.
   a. true
   b. false

5. An RC differentiating circuit has the output taken from across the capacitor.
   a. true
   b. false

6. An integrating circuit has R = 4.7 kΩ in series with C = 0.005 μF. What is the time constant?
   a. 23.5 μs
   b. 2.35 ms
   c. 0.0235 ms
   d. 0.00235 ms

7. An integrating circuit has R = 100 kΩ and C = 22 μF. What is the time constant?
   a. 2.2 ms
   b. 2.2 μs
   c. 2.2 s
   d. 22 s

8. A 5.1-MΩ resistor is in series with a 100-pF capacitor. How long will it take to completely charge the capacitor?
   a. 25.5 s
   b. 2.55 s
   c. 255 ms
   d. 2.55 ms

9. A 100-μF capacitor is charged to 75 V. You discharge it through a 47-kΩ resistor. How long will it take to completely discharge?
   a. 4.7 s
   b. 23.5 s
   c. 47.6 s
   d. 75 s

10. A 12-V pulse is applied to an RC integrator. The pulse width equals one time constant. What will the voltage across the capacitor be at the end of the pulse?
   a. 4.41 V
   b. 12 V
   c. 7.58 V
   d. 0 V

11. An RC integrator circuit has a C = 0.05 μF and R = 22 kΩ. A single pulse of 12 V is applied to the circuit. The pulse width is 2.2 ms. Determine the capacitor voltage at the end of the pulse.
   a. 10.38 V
   b. 12 V
   c. 7.58 V
   d. 4.42 V

12. An RC integrator has C = 47 μF and R = 12 kΩ. A square wave input with a frequency of 200 kHz is applied. The approximate output of the circuit is
   a. a square wave with a frequency of 100 kHz.
   b. 0 V.
   c. a square wave with a frequency of 200 kHz.
   d. a near dc voltage of about half the peak square wave voltage.

13. An RC differentiator circuit has C = 47 μF and R = 12kΩ. The input signal is a square wave with a very short pulse width compared to the time constant. The output signal will be
   a. a dc value of about half the peak input voltage.
   b. a square wave very similar to the input voltage.
   c. a dc voltage level equal to the peak input voltage.
   d. zero volts.

14. An RL integrator has the output taken _________ the _________.
   a. across, resistor
   b. across, inductor
   c. across, resistor and inductor
   d. in parallel with, inductor

15. You want to fully charge a 200 μF capacitor in 12 s. What size resistor should you use?
   a. 60 kΩ
   b. 12 kΩ
   c. 6 kΩ
   d. 1.2 kΩ

16. A 47-μF capacitor is in series with a 12-kΩ resistor. A pulse of 12 V is applied for 2.256 s. What is the voltage across the capacitor?
   a. 7.58 V
   b. 10.38 V
   c. 11.4 V
   d. 12 V

17. An RL integrator circuit has L = 10 mH and R = 10 Ω. A pulse with a peak voltage of 16 V is applied for 1 ms. What is the output voltage?
   a. 10.11 V
   b. 13.84 V
   c. 15.2 V
   d. 16.32 V

18. An RL integrator has R = 25 Ω and L = 200 μH. A pulse with a peak voltage of 25 V is applied for 16 μs. What is the output voltage?
   a. 15.63 V
   b. 21.63 V
   c. 23.75 V
   d. 25 V

19. You decide to compare an RC integrator to an RL integrator. You put the same square wave signal into both circuits. The results
   a. indicate opposite action.
   b. indicate a higher voltage out from the RC integrator.
   c. indicate a higher voltage out from the RL integrator.
   d. indicate the exact same output from both circuits.

20. An RC integrator circuit can be used for
   a. obtaining good dc output.
   b. wave shaping input waveforms.
   c. timing circuits with pulse inputs.
   d. all of the above.

REVIEW OF KEY POINTS IN CHAPTER 17

INTRODUCTION TO SEMICONDUCTOR DEVICES

INTRODUCTION TO SEMICONDUCTORS

- Negatively charged electrons orbit the positively charged nucleus of an atom.
- The electrons in the outermost shell of an atom are called **valence electrons**.
- In some atoms valence electrons can easily be removed from the outer shell and become free electrons.
- Free electrons are able to jump to the outer shell of another atom.
- Two widely used semiconductor materials are silicon and germanium. (These are called <u>semi</u>conductor materials because their valence shell contains four electrons out of a complete shell of eight electrons.)
- Atoms of silicon form themselves into a covalent bond. These atoms share the valence electrons.
- Silicon molecules are called crystals.
- When an electron becomes a free electron and moves away from the atom, a hole exists.
- For every free electron, there is a hole.
- In silicon the electrons are excited into becoming free by light or thermal energy.
- When a voltage is applied across a piece of silicon, the free electrons are attracted by the positive side of the source.
- This movement of free electrons is called **electron current**.
- The apparent movement of the holes left by the free electrons is called **hole current**.
- Silicon semiconductor material is doped to modify the number of electrons in the material.

- N-type semiconductors are doped to have more electrons than pure silicon. N means negative, hence more electrons.
- P-type semiconductors are doped to have fewer electrons than pure silicon. P means less negative or positive. P also means more holes.

PN JUNCTIONS

- If a chip of silicon is doped so half is N-type material and the other half is P-type material, a PN junction is formed between the materials.
- A common name for a PN junction is a diode.
- Where the PN junction combines, a depletion layer is formed. The voltage across this barrier is about 0.7 V for silicon and 0.3 V for germanium.
- If the temperature increases, the barrier voltage decreases and vice versa.

DIODE BIAS

- A diode is considered forward-biased if the forward voltage across the PN junction is about 0.7 V. This means that the P or positive part of the junction must be positive by 0.7 V as compared to the N-material.
- When a diode is forward-biased, current will flow across the junction.
- Reverse bias means that the junction blocks the flow of current through it.
- The polarity of reverse-bias voltages is opposite to forward bias.
- There is a small reverse leakage current across a reverse-biased diode. This current is usually very small.
- Reverse breakdown occurs if the reverse voltage is great enough to force current through the diode in the reverse direction. This is damaging in most conditions.

- When a diode is forward-biased, an attempt to increase the potential will only cause more current to flow. The forward voltage across the diode will remain at about 0.7 V for silicon.

- A simple comparison to a diode is a switch. If the switch is open, no current flows. If the diode is reverse-biased, no current flows. The opposite is also true.

TECHNICIAN TIPS

- A diode has two terminals, a positive or anode (the P-type material) and a negative or cathode (the N-type material). One end of small diodes is usually marked with a black band. This is the cathode end. Most diodes are marked by their part number printed on them. Diodes are characterized by a number that starts with 1N. The following numbers indicate the particular diode type: 1N3904.

- Bias in electronics means the dc voltage that sets the operating condition of the semiconductor device. If the forward voltage across a diode is about 0.7 V, it is conducting or "on." If the voltage across the diode is negative, then the diode is reverse-biased or "off." The relative polarity between the anode and cathode are all that is considered in determining the state of a diode. The actual voltage level is of no concern.

- A diode can be tested with an ohmmeter. Connect the positive lead of the meter to the anode of the diode and a low value of resistance should be read. Reverse the meter leads, and a high value of resistance should be read. Most digital multimeters (DMM) have a diode check position that will supply the voltage to forward-bias the diode. If the two readings are low, the diode is shorted. If both readings are high, the diode is open. Replace it in either case.

CHAPTER 17 QUIZ

Student Name ____

1. Silicon and germanium are semiconductor materials.
   a. true
   b. false

2. Doping is adding impurities to semiconductor materials to obtain some desired characteristics.
   a. true
   b. false

3. A forward-biased diode prevents current from flowing.
   a. true
   b. false

4. Reverse breakdown occurs when a diode is reverse-biased by 0.7 V.
   a. true
   b. false

5. The barrier potential is the inherent voltage across the depletion layer.
   a. true
   b. false

6. The smallest particle of an element that retains the characteristics of that element is called a/an __________.
   a. ion
   b. electron
   c. atom
   d. molecule

7. A conduction band electron is called a/an __________.
   a. free electron
   b. atom
   c. positive ion
   d. negative ion

8. Reverse leakage current is due to _______________.
   a. a forward voltage across the diode
   b. thermal runaway
   c. depletion layer breakdown
   d. thermally produced electron-hole pairs

9. You measure the voltage across a diode and it measures 17 V. The diode is considered ________________.
   a. forward-biased
   b. reverse-biased
   c. in heavy conduction
   d. none of these

10. You test a diode for proper operation by placing the leads of an ohmmeter + to the anode and - to the cathode of the diode. This should give you a ________ resistance.
   a. very high
   b. zero
   c. low reading of
   d. reading of 140 kΩ

11. A silicon diode is in series with a 1-kΩ resistor across a 12-V source. The diode is forward-biased. The voltage across the diode is________ and across the resistor is ________.
   a. 0.3 V, 11.7 V
   b. 0.7 V, 12 V
   c. 0.3 V, 11.3 V
   d. 0.7 V, 11.3 V

12. A silicon diode is in a series circuit. You measure the voltage from the anode to ground and it measures 0.4 V. You believe the diode is forward-biased. What voltage should you measure between the cathode and ground for a forward-bias condition?
   a. 0.7 V
   b. -0.3 V
   c. -0.7 V
   d. 1.7 V

13. To forward-bias a silicon diode with a voltage to ground of -17 V on the anode, a voltage of ________ is required on the cathode.
   a. -17.7 V
   b. -16.3 V
   c. -17.3 V
   d. -16.7 V

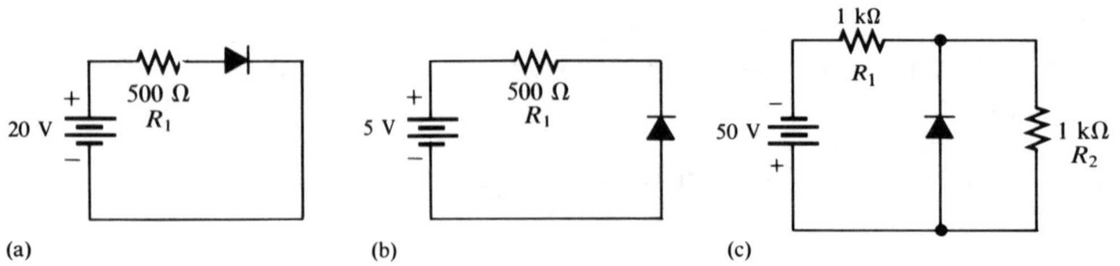

FIGURE 17-1

14. See Figure 17-1(a). If the diode is germanium, what is the voltage across the diode?
   a. 20 V
   b. 19.3 V
   c. 19.7 V
   d. 0.3 V

15. See Figure 17-1(b). If the diode is silicon, the circuit current is ________.
   a. 10 mA
   b. 100 A
   c. 9.4 mA
   d. 0 mA

16. See Figure 17-1(c). The diode is silicon. What is the current through R_2?
   a. 700 µA
   b. 25 mA
   c. 0
   d. 300 µA

17. See Figure 17-1(c). The diode is silicon. What is the voltage drop across R_1?
   a. 50 V
   b. 25 V
   c. 49.3 V
   d. 49.7 V

18. See Figure 17-1(a). If the diode is silicon, what is V_R?
   a. 20.7 V
   b. 20 V
   c. 19.7 V
   d. 19.3 V

19. See Figure 17-1(c). The diode is silicon. What is V_{R2}?
   a. 0.7 V
   b 0.3 V
   c. 25 V
   d. 24.3 V

20. You check a diode with your ohmmeter. The reading is high with both positions of the meter leads. The diode is probably ________.
   a. shorted
   b. open
   c. forward-biased
   d. reverse-biased

REVIEW OF KEY POINTS IN CHAPTER 18

DIODES AND APPLICATIONS

HALF-WAVE RECTIFIERS

- Diodes conduct current in only one direction.
- To rectify is to convert ac to pulsating dc.
- In a half-wave rectifier, the diode will conduct only during the positive alternation. This will give a series of half-waves of positive pulsating dc.
- A dc voltmeter will read the average of the half-wave output. The formula for this approximate output voltage is $V_{AVG} = V_P/\pi$.
- The actual value for peak voltage is $V_{P(out)} = V_{P(in)} - 0.7$ V.
- PIV (peak inverse voltage) is the maximum reverse voltage the diode can withstand before breaking down.
- When a diode is used in a rectifier, the diode <u>must</u> have a PIV rating in excess of the negative V_P. (A safe practical rating would by 2 x V_P.

FULL-WAVE RECTIFIERS

- A full-wave rectifier will have two diodes. Each diode will alternately conduct, giving a positive output voltage of pulsating dc for each positive and negative alternation.
- The average dc output voltage of a full-wave rectifier is $V_{AVG} = 2V_P/\pi$.
- A full-wave rectifier using two diodes requires a transformer with a center-tapped secondary.
- This transformer reduces the voltage to the load by one-half, since only one half is used in any instant.
- The diodes used in a full-wave rectifier must have a PIV = $2V_{P(out)}$.

FULL-WAVE BRIDGE RECTIFIERS

- To eliminate the need for a center-tapped transformer, four diodes can be used in a bridge circuit.

- $V_{(out)} \approx V_S$. The only error is the forward drop of two diodes in series.

- $PIV \approx V_{P(out)}$.

RECTIFIER FILTERS

- The output from a half-wave rectifier is pulsating dc with a frequency equal to the supply frequency.

- The output from either type of full-wave rectifier is pulsating dc with a frequency of twice the supply frequency.

- This pulsating dc must be smoothed out to a good dc level with small varying voltages.

- A low-pass filter is usually used to smooth the dc.

- A capacitor across the rectifier output will provide basic filtering action.

- The resulting variations in the dc output from charging and discharging the capacitor is called **ripple.** The lower the ripple voltage, the better the filtering action.

- To decrease the ripple voltage, increase the size of the filter capacitor.

- A low-pass filter using an inductor as the input is sometimes used.

- A π-type filter using two capacitors and one inductor is also used.

DIODE CLIPPING CIRCUITS

- Clipping circuits is sometimes called **limiting circuits.**

- Since a diode will conduct only when it is forward-biased, a clipping action will occur if an ac signal is applied to a diode parallel to the load.

- This output is similar to the output from a half-wave rectifier.

- The clipping level can be changed by adding a dc voltage in series with the diode.

- Many combinations of output clipped waveforms are possible by changing the positions of the diode and/or the polarity of the series dc voltage.

- Clipping is used to clip portions of signals for use in other parts of a circuit.

DIODE CLAMPING CIRCUITS

- Clamping circuits are also called **dc restorers**.

- Clamping circuits insert a dc level, either positive or negative, into a signal.

- To work properly, the capacitor must be large or the load must have a high resistance to keep from discharging the capacitor between cycles. This high load resistance provides a high RC time constant.

- The amount of dc voltage can be controlled by inserting a dc source in series with the diode.

ZENER DIODES

- A zener diode is used in voltage-regulating circuits.

- A zener diode will breakdown or avalanche if the reverse voltage applied to it exceeds the zener voltage, V_Z.

- The zener diode is built so that it will maintain a constant voltage across it when it has avalanched.

- By connecting small loads in parallel with the zener diode, the load voltage is regulated.

- Zeners come in voltage ratings of 1.8 V to 200 V.

- Zener diodes have limited power or current ratings.

- A series current limiting resistor must always be used with zener diodes.
- In a voltage regulator circuit using a zener diode, if the load resistance decreases, I_L increases and I_Z decreases. The opposite is true if I_L decreases.

VARACTOR DIODES

- Varactor diodes are used as voltage-variable capacitors.
- Varactor diodes have values from a few picofarads to a few hundred picofarads.
- Varactor diodes are reverse-biased PN junctions whose capacitance varies inversely with an increase in reverse voltage.
- Electronic tuners in TVs, radios, and other communication receivers use varactor diodes.

LEDs AND PHOTODIODES

- A light-emitting diode, LED, will emit light according to the forward voltage applied to it.
- LEDs come in a variety of colors according to the semiconductor materials used.
- The uses for LEDs are as indicating lights for an infinite variety of equipment.
- A photodiode is a reverse-bias PN junction device that conducts more current as the light intensity upon it increases.
- The internal resistance varies from very high with no light to a low value resistance with bright light on the junction.
- The device is built so light can shine on the junction within the device.

TECHNICIAN TIPS

- Full-wave bridge rectifiers are used extensively. Many times four separate diodes are used. However, manufacturers have encapsulated the four diodes into one package. This package comes in a variety of ratings. There are just four terminals, two input and two output. With this package, if one diode fails, you must replace the entire package.

- Students are often called upon to draw the schematic diagram of a full-wave bridge rectifier. Some confusion can occur in the correct placing of the diodes in the diagram. A tip to remember is this: To obtain a positive output voltage, all four diodes should have their arrows pointing to the right. Negative voltages would require the opposite.

- An important troubleshooting tool in power supplies is the ripple voltage. You must turn the scope V/cm to more amplification to see the ripple. Make sure you have the scope set to the ac input. A high peak-to-peak ripple voltage could indicate a leaky or open filter capacitor. A change in the ripple frequency could indicate a failure of one of the diodes, causing the rectifier to become a half-wave rectifier. Remember, ripple frequency for a full-wave rectifier output is twice the line input frequency. The half-wave ripple frequency equals the line frequency.

- If a diode opens, there will be an increase in the ripple voltage and a change of ripple frequency as mentioned above. The average dc voltage will also decrease.

- A shorted diode will cause too much current to flow, possibly damaging the power transformer winding or preferably blowing the fuse.

- If the filter capacitor shorts, no output voltage will occur. Also, this condition will cause some of the diodes to fail due to excessive current. An open filter capacitor will cause the ripple to be maximum and the dc voltage to decrease. No filtering action would occur. If the electrolytic filter capacitor becomes leaky, its capacitance would decrease, causing the ripple voltage to increase and the output dc voltage to slightly decrease.

- Diode clipping circuits require a look at the state of the diode during the input waveform cycle. If the diode is off, the output equals the input. If the diode is on, the output voltage equals the voltage across the diode plus any dc voltage in series with the diode. The dc voltage determines the clipping level. Clipping voltages from negative to positive can be obtained as desired. For a shortcut, look at the direction of the diode arrow. If it is pointing up, the circuit will pass all voltages above the clipping level. If it is pointing down, the reverse is true.

- Diode clampers clamp the positive or negative peaks at the clamping voltage. This clamping voltage is determined by the dc source in series with the diode. Another shortcut is if the diode is pointing down, the circuit will clamp the positive peaks at the clamping level. In other words, the waveform is shifted in the direction of the diode arrow.

- A zener diode is used as a reference voltage in many circuits. It is also used as a voltage regulator for small levels of power. In a simple zener regulator circuit, an increase in the load current will cause the zener current to decrease. If I_{RL} decreases, I_Z will increase. If the source voltage increases, the load current will remain the same but the zener current will increase. In this case, the current through the series resistor will also increase. A decrease in V_S will produce opposite changes.

CHAPTER 18 QUIZ

Student Name ____

1. The output frequency of a full-wave rectifier equals the input frequency.
   a. true
   b. false

2. The basic types of full-wave rectifiers are center-tapped and bridge.
   a. true
   b. false

3. Diode clippers cut off voltage above or below specified levels.
   a. true
   b. false

4. A zener diode is used as a variable voltage source.
   a. true
   b. false

5. Ripple voltage is caused by the charging and discharging of the filter capacitor.
   a. true
   b. false

6. A half-wave rectifier has an output of
   a. pulsating dc with a frequency of twice the line frequency.
   b. pure dc.
   c. pulsating dc with a frequency equal to the line frequency.
   d. only negative pulses of voltage.

7. A half-wave rectifier has an output of 38 V_p. The PIV of the diode should be more than __________.
   a. 76 V
   b. 38 V
   c. 27 V
   d. 19 V

8. The average output of a full-wave rectifier with a peak value of 169 V is ________.
   a. 53.79 V
   b. 239 V
   c. 119 48 V
   d. 107.59 V

9. A full-wave bridge rectifier requires
   a. a center-tapped transformer.
   b. four diodes and a transformer with a single secondary.
   c. two diodes and a transformer with a single secondary.
   d. a high voltage to operate it.

10. A typical ripple voltage from a good power supply
   a. is very low.
   b. is very high.
   c. varies from small to large.
   d. is about 1 V_{p-p}.

11. If the diode in a half-wave rectifier opens,
   a. the output ripple would be very large.
   b. the output voltage would equal the ac input voltage.
   c. the output voltage would be zero.
   d. the output voltage would not change.

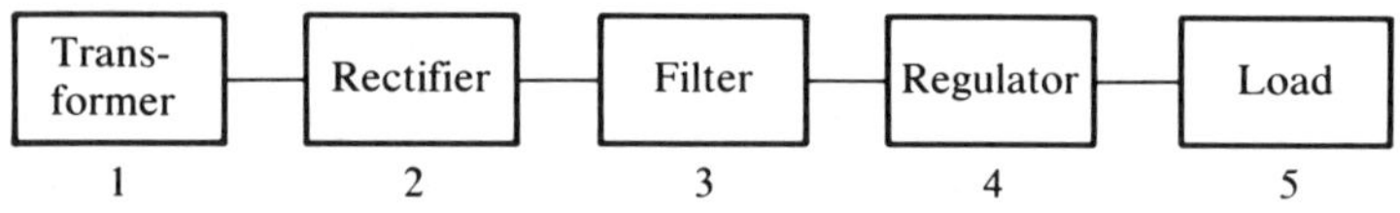

FIGURE 18-1

12. See Figure 18-1. What is the purpose of block #1?
   a. changes ac to pulsating dc
   b. changes the amplitude of the ac
   c. smooths the pulsating dc
   d. regulates the dc output

13. See Figure 18-1. What is the purpose of block #3?
   a. changes ac to pulsating dc
   b. changes the amplitude of the ac
   c. smoothes the pulsating dc
   d. regulates the dc output

14. See Figure 18-1. What is the purpose of block #2?
   a. changes ac to pulsating dc
   b. changes the amplitude of the ac
   c. smoothes the pulsating dc
   d. regulates the dc output

15. If a diode in the full-wave rectifier opens, the output
   a. dc voltage will decrease and the ripple voltage will decrease.
   b. dc voltage will increase and the ripple frequency will decrease.
   c. dc voltage will increase and the ripple voltage will decrease.
   d. dc voltage will decrease and the ripple frequency will decrease.

16. See Figure 18-1. If the filter capacitor shorts,
    a. the output voltage will be zero.
    b. the output voltage will be ac.
    c. the ripple voltage will be very high.
    d. the voltage regulator will break down.

17. See Figure 18-1. If the filter capacitor becomes leaky,
    a. the output dc will decrease and the ripple voltage will decrease.
    b. the output dc will increase and the ripple voltage will increase.
    c. the output dc will remain the same but the diodes will fail.
    d. the ripple voltage will increase and the dc output will decrease.

18. See Figure 18-1. The purpose of block #4 is
    a. to adjust the output voltage to the correct ac value.
    b. to keep the dc output voltage constant as the load changes.
    c. to make sure that the fuse will not blow.
    d. to maintain a constant output current when the load current changes.

19. In a simple zener regulator circuit, if the load current increases, then
    a. the total current will increase.
    b. the current through the series resistor will increase.
    c. the voltage across the series resistor will decrease.
    d. the zener current will decrease.

20. In a simple zener regulator circuit, if the source voltage increases, then
    a. the load current also will increase.
    b. the voltage across the zener will increase.
    c. the voltage across the series resistor will decrease.
    d. the zener current will increase.

REVIEW OF KEY POINTS IN CHAPTER 19

TRANSISTORS AND THYRISTORS

BIPOLAR JUNCTION TRANSISTORS

- A bipolar junction transistor (BJT) has two PN junctions, the base-emitter junction and the base-collector junction.
- The base-emitter junction is forward-biased and the base-collector junction is reverse-biased.
- The BJT can be an NPN-type or a PNP-type. The NPN refers to the doping of the collector, base, and emitter with either N- or P-type material. The PNP is the opposite.
- If the junctions are correctly biased, then current flow can be amplified. I_B is the base current, I_C is the collector current, and I_E is the emitter current. $I_E = I_B + I_C$.
- The dc current gain is represented by beta (β). $\beta = I_C/I_B$.
- Voltages are measured from each element to ground. There is the emitter voltage V_E, the collector voltage V_C, and the base voltage V_B.
- A common bias arrangement to provide the proper dc voltages is voltage divider bias.
- The input resistance of a BJT with voltage divider bias is about $R_{IN} = \beta_{dc}R_E$.

THE BJT TRANSISTOR IN AMPLIFIERS

- The purpose of dc bias is to allow a transistor to operate as an amplifier.
- An amplifier is a circuit that will produce a much larger output than the input.
- Transistors operate on a set of curves called characteristic curves. There is set of these curves for each type of transistor.
- The operating or Q point is the place on the characteristic curves that the dc bias values will force the transistor to operate.

- A transistor can be operating in cutoff, saturation, or anywhere in between.
- A transistor operating in cutoff has $I_B = 0$.
- Saturation is a condition where an increase in I_B will no longer cause a corresponding increase in I_C. V_{CE} is almost zero.
- A signal applied to the base causes I_C to change, allowing V_C to change. This change in I_{C1} develops a voltage across R_C.
- The output voltage at the collector is 180° out of phase with the input voltage at the base.
- The approximate voltage gain of this amplifier is $A_V = R_C/R_E$.

THE BJT AS A SWITCH

- If a BJT is operating in cutoff, the output voltage at the collector is V_{CC}. The output current is zero, so the switch is off.
- A BJT operating in a saturation condition has a $V_{CE} = 0$. Since the output current is maximum, the switch is on.
- This operation of transistors as a switch is used extensively in digital logic circuits.

BJT PARAMETERS

- β varies directly with temperature. If the temperature increases, β increases. This increase can cause a change of gain for an amplifier.
- Maximum ratings for a transistor are given in the manufacturer's data sheet. Maximum ratings are given for V_{CB}, V_{CE}, V_{EB}, I_C, and I_B.
- An important maximum rating also given is power dissipation P_D.
- The maximum power dissipation is $P_D = V_{CE}/I_C$.

JUNCTION FIELD EFFECT TRANSISTORS

- JFETs are of two types: N-channel and P-channel.
- The junction between the gate and the source is reverse-biased.
- The amount of drain current is controlled by the gate-source voltage V_{GS}. As V_{GS} becomes more negative, the drain current decreases.
- The JFET is a voltage-controlled device.
- As V_{GS} is made more negative, the drain current decreases until it is at a minimum value. This is V_P, pinch-off.
- The input resistance of a JFET is very high, typically up to 20,000 MΩ.

METAL OXIDE SEMICONDUCTOR FET (MOSFET)

- The MOSFET comes in two types, depletion-enhancement (DE) and enhancement-only (E).
- The MOSFET has no junction. The gate is insulated from the channel by a thin layer of silicon dioxide.
- The value of V_{GS} in a DE MOSFET can be either positive or negative.
- The E MOSFET requires a positive value of V_{GS} to form the channel so drain current can flow.
- The input resistance of a MOSFET is extremely high.
- MOSFETs can be destroyed by static electricity in simple handling. Special care should be exercised when handling MOSFETs. Good grounding practices must be observed.

FET BIASING

- A simple bias arrangement for a JFET is a self-bias circuit. The gate is at 0 V. The negative bias required of V_{GS} is obtained by use of a source resistor.

- Depletion-enhancement MOSFETs also can be self-biased with V_{GS} at 0 V.

- Enhancement-only MOSFETs can use a voltage divider type of bias.

UNIJUNCTION TRANSISTOR

- A unijunction transistor UJT has an emitter and two bases.

- The operation of the UJT depends on the forward voltage of the emitter-$base_1$ junction. If this junction is forward-biased, the UJT conducts.

- The UJT is not an amplifier. It is a bistable device or switch.

- A common use for the UJT is in oscillator circuits. Another use is in control circuits.

THYRISTORS

- Thyristors are a family of four-layer devices. They are primarily used in control circuits, such as, lamp-dimming circuits, motor speed control, ignition circuits, and electric railway controls.

- As a family, they are open-circuit devices until a trigger or gate voltage is applied. They then conduct even though the trigger voltage is removed.

- They can be turned off by interrupting the supply voltage or in some types by a trigger voltage.

- A silicon-controlled rectifier (SCR), can be turned on by a positive voltage at the gate. Once conducting it will remain on as long as the current remains above the minimum holding current value.

- An SCR will conduct only on positive alternations.

- A triac is a device with essentially two SCRs so it will conduct on either positive or negative alternations. It is also turned on by a positive pulse applied to the gate.

- A diac is a device that will conduct in either direction. It does not have a gate. It is triggered by the voltage across the terminals in either direction.
- A diac is often used to trigger a triac.

TECHNICIAN TIPS

- BJT transistors are operated with the correct bias. The BE junction is forward-biased and the BC junction is reverse-biased. This is true if either a PNP or NPN transistor is used. If your BJT is biased correctly, then the dc voltage on the collector should be about 1/2 V_{CC}. This will be correct for many amplifier applications.
- The use of a BJT as a switch is common. Be sure you understand that in cutoff, $V_C = V_{CC}$. In saturation, remember $V_{CE} = 0$. Actually, V_{CE} will be a few tenths of a volt up to one volt at saturation.
- Cutoff and saturation conditions are useful troubleshooting conditions because just a few voltage measurements are required. A lot of amplifier problems can be found using these three measurements, V_C, V_B, and V_E. If $V_C = V_{CC}$, then $I_C = 0$. You must then determine which component has failed. Remember cutoff and saturation.
- Transistors can be checked with an ohmmeter. Recall the method to check a diode. The BJT is a two-junction device. Measure the BE junction with the ohmmeter. The reading will be high or low depending on the lead polarity. Also, check the BC junction. Lastly, check the resistance between the emitter and collector. It should be high with either position of the leads.

CHAPTER 19 QUIZ

Student Name ______________________________

1. The two types of BJT are the NPN and the P-channel.
   a. true
   b. false

2. A BJT has three elements: emitter, base, and collector.
   a. true
   b. false

3. JFET current flows between the source and the drain through a channel whose conductive width is controlled by the amount of reverse bias on the gate-source junction.
   a. true
   b. false

4. An enhancement-only MOSFET can only operate with a negative value of V_{GS}.
   a. true
   b. false

5. Transistors can be used as amplifiers or switches.
   a. true
   b. false

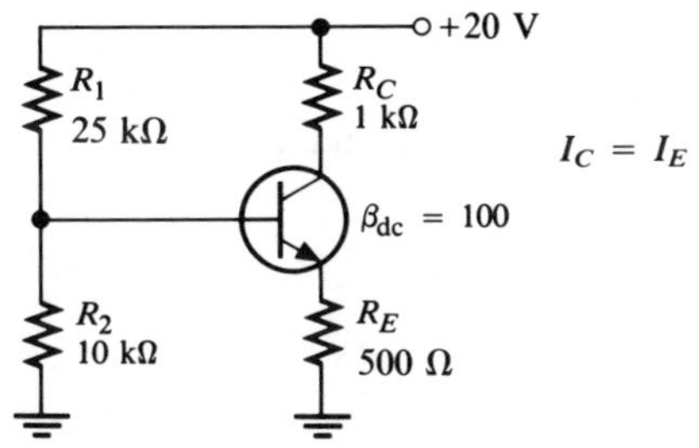

FIGURE 19-1

6. See Figure 19-1. Find V_B.
   a. 5.7 V
   b. 14.3 V
   c. 5 V
   d. 4.3 V

7. See Figure 19-1. Find V_E.
   a. 5.7 V
   b. 5 V
   c. 13.6 V
   d. 3.6 V

8. See Figure 19-1. Find I_C.
   a. 11.4 mA
   b. 27.2 mA
   c. 10 mA
   d. 7.2 mA

9. See Figure 19-1. Find V_C.
   a. 20 V
   b. 5.71 V
   c. 5 V
   d. 10 V

10. See Figure 19-1. Find V_{CE}.
   a. 11.4 V
   b. 5 V
   c. 6.4 V
   d. 16.4 V

11. See Figure 19-1. Find I_B.
   a. 114 μA
   b. 272 μA
   c. 7.2 μA
   d. 100 μA

12. See Figure 19-1. Which of the following voltages might indicate if this amplifier was in saturation?
   a. $V_C = 20$ V
   b. $V_{CE} = 20$ V
   c. $V_{CE} = 0$ V
   d. $V_{BE} = 0.5$ V

13. See Figure 19-1. Which of the following voltages might indicate if this amplifier was cutoff?
   a. $V_C = 20$ V
   b. $V_{CE} = 0$ V
   c. $V_E = 20$ V
   d. $V_{BE} = 0.7$ V

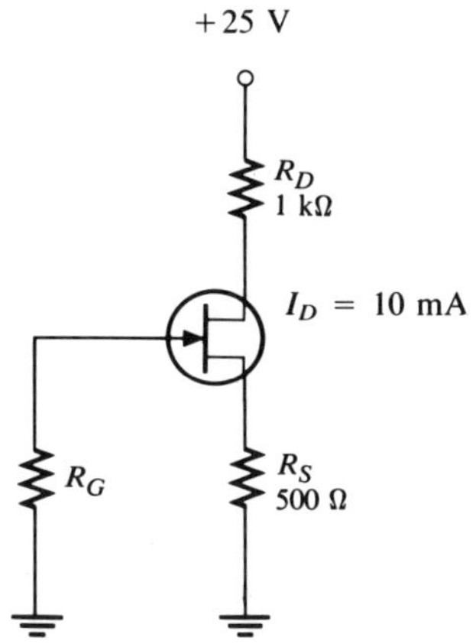

FIGURE 19-2

14. See Figure 19-2. Find V_S.
    a. 15 V
    b. 12 V
    c. 5 V
    d. 0 V

15. See Figure 19-2. Find V_D.
    a. 15 V
    b. 10 V
    c. 5 V
    d. 0 V

16. See Figure 19-2. Find V_{GS}.
    a. 5 V
    b. -5 V
    c. -10 V
    d. 10 V

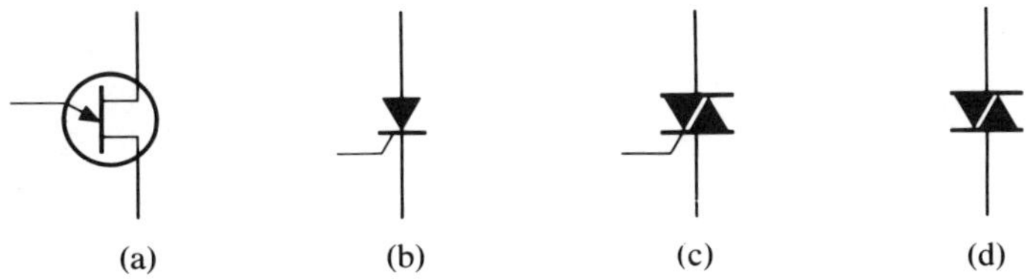

FIGURE 19-3

17. See Figure 19-3. Which symbol represents a triac?
    a. a
    b. b
    c. c
    d. d

18. See Figure 19-3(a). This symbol represents a/an
a. diac
b. N-channel JFET
c. MOSFET
d. UJT

19. See Figure 19-3. Which symbol represents a diac?
a. a
b. b
c. c
d. d

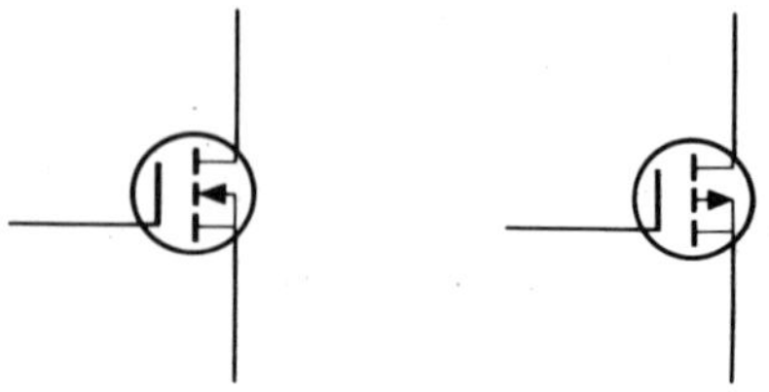
(a) (b)

FIGURE 19-4

20. See Figure 19-4(a). This symbol represents a/an
a. N-channel depletion-enhancement JFET.
b. P-channel enhancement-only MOSFET.
c. N-channel enhancement-only MOSFET.
d. N-channel enhancement-only JFET.

REVIEW OF KEY POINTS IN CHAPTER 20

AMPLIFIERS AND OSCILLATORS

COMMON-EMITTER AMPLIFIER

- The common-emitter (CE) amplifier is an amplifier using a BJT with the input signal on the base and the output signal taken from the collector.
- The unused element for signal input or output will always indicate the type of configuration.
- The addition of an emitter bypass capacitor will increase the ac voltage gain of the amplifier. The emitter is then operating at ac ground potential.
- The internal emitter resistance (r_e) of a transistor is found by $r_e = 25\ mV/I_E$.
- The voltage gain of a CE amplifier with an emitter bypass capacitor is given by $A_V = R_C/r_e$.
- The output voltage from a CE amplifier is 180° out of phase with the input voltage.
- The input resistance ($R_{in(T)}$) to the circuit is R_1, R_2, and $\beta_{ac}r_e$ all in parallel.
- $I_s = V_s/R_{in(T)}$.
- The current gain is found by $A_i = I_C/I_s$.
- The power gain is found by $A_p = A_vA_i$.
- Gains can be expressed in decibels.

COMMON-COLLECTOR AMPLIFIER

- The common-collector (CC) amplifier has the input at the base and the output taken from the emitter.
- The CC amplifier is also called an emitter-follower. This is because the output at the emitter follows the input at the base.
- The voltage gain is approximately 1.

- The output voltage is in phase with the input voltage.
- The input resistance is much higher than the CE.
- The power gain is about equal to the current gain.
- The Darlington pair amplifier is a two-stage, direct coupled, CC amplifier.
- The current gain is $\beta_{DARL} = \beta_1\beta_2$.
- The input impedance is $\beta_{DARL}R_E$.

COMMON-BASE AMPLIFIER

- The common-base (CB) amplifier has the input signal on the emitter and the output taken from the collector.
- The voltage gain $A_v = R_C/r_e$. This is the same as for the CE when R_E is bypassed.
- The current gain is approximately 1.
- The power gain is about equal to the voltage gain.
- The output voltage at the collector is in phase with the input voltage at the emitter.

THE FET COMMON-SOURCE AMPLIFIER

- A common-source (CS) amplifier has the input signal on the gate and the output taken from the drain.
- A CS amplifier can use a source bypass capacitor to increase the voltage gain.
- The output voltage at the drain is 180° out of phase with the input voltage at the gate.
- The transconductance (g_m) is specified in the data sheets for an FET.
- The voltage gain of a CS amplifier is given by $A_v = g_mR_D$.
- The input impedance of a CS amplifier is very high.
- MOSFETs can also be connected in a CS configuration.

THE FET COMMON-DRAIN AMPLIFIER

- A common-drain (CD) amplifier uses an FET with the input signal on the gate and the output taken from the source.
- Another name for the CD amplifier is source-follower.
- The voltage gain of the CD amplifier is about 1.
- The input impedance of the CD amplifier is essentially R_G.
- The output voltage is in phase with the input voltage.

MULTISTAGE AMPLIFIERS

- Several amplifiers can be connected in cascade, with output of one stage driving the next stage.
- The voltage gain of a multistage amplifier is found by $A_{VT} = A_{V1}A_{V2}A_{V3} \cdots A_{Vn}$.
- Voltage gain is often expressed in dB. A_V (dB) = 20 log A_V.
- The voltage gain in dB of several stages of amplification can be found by adding the individual stage gains in dB.
- Another amplifier added to the output of any amplifier will load the first stage. This will produce a reduced voltage gain in the first stage.

CLASS A OPERATION

- An amplifier that is biased to operate in the linear region where the output signal is an amplified version of the input signal is operating class A.
- The Q point is centered on the load line so signal swings can be maximum without driving the amplifier into either cutoff or saturation.
- The efficiency of a class A amplifier is about 25%.
- Collector current is flowing during the entire signal cycle.

CLASS B PUSH-PULL OPERATION

- An amplifier biased so that it conducts only half or 180° of the cycle is operating class B.
- In a push-pull amplifier, each transistor is on half the time.
- The maximum efficiency is 78.5%. Typical efficiencies achieved are closer to 50%.
- Crossover distortion occurs when a push-pull amplifier is biased at cutoff. Adding a small amount of forward bias will eliminate much of this distortion.

CLASS C OPERATION

- A class C amplifier is biased so conduction occurs over much less than half the cycle.
- Tuned amplifiers with tank circuits use class C amplifiers at radio frequencies. The tank circuit smoothes out the distorted pulse applied to it by the class C amplifier. This results in a fair quality sine wave output.
- The efficiency of class C amplifiers is quite high.

OSCILLATORS

- An **oscillator** is a circuit that will provide an ac signal at a particular frequency. There is no externally applied signal.
- An oscillator is an amplifier that provides its own input through a feedback network.
- The feedback network must provide positive or in-phase feedback.
- The amplifier must provide enough gain to overcome the feedback loss.
- An RC oscillator provides the positive feedback through a network of resistors and capacitors that shifts to signal the correct amount.

- The Colpitts oscillator uses a tank circuit to provide the necessary feedback and to establish the operating resonant frequency.

- A Hartley oscillator is similar to the Colpitts except the feedback is through two inductors and a capacitor.

- Another basic oscillator is the Clapp. It is similar to the Colpitts except there is an additional series capacitor in the tank circuit.

- A crystal oscillator uses the mechanical oscillations of a quartz crystal to provide the correct feedback.

- A quartz crystal exhibits a piezoelectric effect. If a force is applied to the crystal, it will vibrate at a resonant frequency and produce a voltage across the crystal. Conversely, if a pulse of voltage is applied to a crystal, it will vibrate at its natural resonant frequency.

TECHNICIAN TIPS

- A class A common-emitter amplifier has a very high power gain. It is used much more than any other type of BJT amplifier. A good approximation for the input impedance of a CE amplifier with the emitter at ac ground is to use the value of 1 kΩ. Applying the voltage gain formula and using this approximation, the gain becomes $A_V = \beta R_C/1\ k\Omega$.

- A common-source JFET amplifier is biased so V_{GS} is negative. A good rule of thumb is to arrange the resistor values so that $V_{GS} = V_P/2$. Also arrange for I_D to be $I_D = I_{DSS}/2$. These values will place the operating point in the center of the linear range for the JFET.

- Class B push-pull amplifiers are efficient. This higher efficiency comes from the fact that you can allow the collector current of a transistor to be quite large if you can arrange for it to cool down before the heat does damage. The push-pull amplifier does this. Only one transistor is conducting at a time allowing the other transistor to cool off. The complementary type of push-pull amplifier utilizes a pair of matched PNP-NPN transistors. This pair of power transistors is usually mounted on a heat sink. This heat sink removes the excess heat in a similar fashion to a car radiator. The biasing diodes are also usually mounted on the same heat sink so that all the semiconductor characteristics change at about the same rate. This tends to keep the bias voltages where they belong as the temperature changes.

- The signal tracing method of troubleshooting an amplifier is handy. By means of an oscilloscope you can determine the presence of a good signal or lack of a signal. Move the scope input from point to point through the circuit. If you know the proper operation, you can tell if the signal is not correct. When you have isolated the faulty stage of the amplifier, then use the dc operating voltages to determine the possible cause of the trouble. After you have replaced the faulty component, always recheck for proper operation.

- Recognizing oscillators can be easier if you remember these tips. A Hartley oscillator has a tank circuit with the feedback path from a tap on the inductor in the tank or between two inductors in the tank. A Colpitts oscillator has the feedback path from between two capacitors in the tank circuit. A Clapp oscillator is similar to the Colpitts except with the addition of a series capacitor in the tank.

CHAPTER 20 QUIZ

Student Name ______________________________

1. The general characteristics of a common-emitter amplifier are high voltage gain, high current gain, very high power gain, and low input impedance.
   a. true
   b. false

2. The overall gain of a multistage amplifier is the sum of the individual stage gains.
   a. true
   b. false

3. A voltage gain of 1 is a characteristic of a common-base amplifier.
   a. true
   b. false

4. Voltage gain is the ratio of output voltage to input voltage.
   a. true
   b. false

5. An oscillator is an amplifier that provides its own input.
   a. true
   b. false

6. A class A amplifier conducts
   a. for a small portion of the input cycle.
   b. for 180° of the input cycle.
   c. for 360° of the input cycle.
   d. for only 10° of the input cycle.

7. You have a requirement for an amplifier with a high input resistance and a low output resistance. The amplifier to choose would be
   a. a common-emitter.
   b. a common-base.
   c. a common-collector.
   d. a common-gate.

8. A three stage amplifier has these individual stage voltage gains: 12, 154, and 1. What is the total voltage gain of the three stages?
   a. 1848
   b. 167
   c. 166
   d. 12

9. A three-stage amplifier has these individual stage voltage gains: 12, 154, and 1. What type of amplifier might you find used in the third stage?
   a. a common-emitter amplifier
   b. a common-source amplifier
   c. a common-base amplifier
   d. a common-drain amplifier

10. You have a requirement for an amplifier to have a low input resistance and a high output resistance. Which type of amplifier should be used?
   a. common-collector
   b. common-base
   c. common-source
   d. common-emitter

11. You have a requirement for an amplifier to have the input and output signals in phase. Which type of amplifier should be used?
   a. common-emitter
   b. common-source
   c. Hartley amplifier
   d. common-collector

12. Which of the following amplifiers would be used to provide a high voltage gain?
   a. common-emitter
   b. source-follower
   c. common-collector
   d. emitter-follower

13. See Figure 20-1. Which voltage would enable this circuit to operate with little distortion?
   a. $V_{BC} = 9$ V
   b. $V_C = 18$ V
   c. $V_{CE} = 9$ V
   d. $V_{BE} = 7$ V

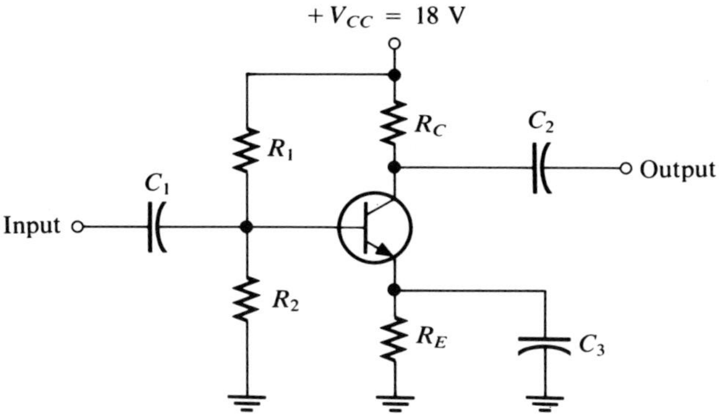

FIGURE 20-1

14. See Figure 20-1. Which voltage would indicate that this amplifier is operating in cutoff?
    a. V_{BC} = 9 V
    b. V_C = 18 V
    c. V_{CE} = 9 V
    d. V_{BE} = 7 V

15. A push-pull amplifier has crossover distortion. It can be reduced
    a. by adding a little reverse bias.
    b. by adding some diodes in the collector circuit.
    c. by adding some forward bias.
    d. by biasing the amplifier below cutoff.

16. A class C amplifier is biased ________ ________ and is used primarily at ________ ________.
    a. at saturation, radio frequencies
    b. below cutoff, radio frequencies
    c. below cutoff, audio frequencies
    d. at cutoff, radio frequencies

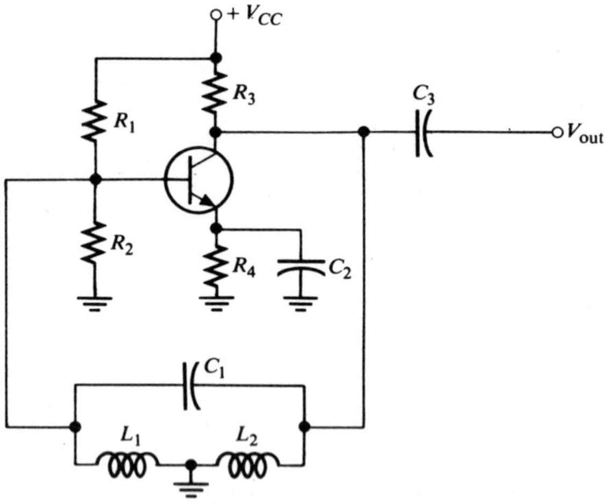

FIGURE 20-2

17. See Figure 20-2. This circuit is known as
    a. a Colpitts oscillator.
    b. a Clapp oscillator.
    c. a Hartley oscillator.
    d. a crystal oscillator.

18. See Figure 20-2. L_1, L_2, and C_1 form a _______ _________, that provides __________ feedback to the amplifier.
    a. tank circuit, positive
    b. feedback network, negative
    c. tank circuit, negative
    d. tank circuit, out-of-phase

19. A Colpitts oscillator can be recognized
    a. by a tapped inductor in the tank.
    b. by a tapped inductor in the collector circuit.
    c. by the feedback from between two capacitors.
    d. by two capacitors in the collector circuit.

20. A crystal oscillator uses a crystal
    a. in place of a tuned Hartley oscillator.
    b. in place of a tank circuit in the feedback network.
    c. in place of the amplifier circuit.
    d. to produce a loud noise in an amplifier.

REVIEW OF KEY POINTS IN CHAPTER 21

OPERATIONAL AMPLIFIERS (OP-AMPS)

OP-AMP INTRODUCTION

- The ideal amplifier has infinite voltage gain, infinite input impedance, zero output impedance, and infinite bandwidth.

- The practical op-amp comes reasonably close to the requirements for an ideal amplifier.

THE DIFFERENTIAL AMPLIFIER

- Differential amplifiers provide high voltage gain and common-mode rejection.

- With one input grounded and a signal applied to the other input, two equal and out of phase signals will be found at the two outputs. This is called single-ended operation.

- If two input signals of opposite polarity are applied, one to each input, the output will be two out-of-phase signals. This is called differential operation.

- Common-mode operation is the input of two equal and in-phase signals to each input. The output signals are near zero.

- Common-mode rejection ratio, CMRR, is the op-amp's ability to reject in-phase signals and amplify out-of-phase signals. In-phase signals are commonly noise or other types of interference.

- CMRR is usually expressed in dB. A value of 80 dB is typical.

OP-AMP DATA SHEET PARAMETERS

- Input offset voltage, V_{OS}, is the differential input voltage required to make the differential output to zero. Typical values are 2 mV. The ideal is zero volts.

- The input offset voltage drift is the specified change in V_{OS} for a change in temperature.

- Input bias current is the current required to operate the input transistors. Typical values are about 80 nA.

- The input impedance is listed at around 2 mΩ. Actual values much greater than this figure are achieved due to circuit configurations.

- The input offset current is the difference between the two input bias currents. Small values of 20 nA are typical.

- Output impedance is typically listed in data sheets at around 75 Ω. Actual values less than this are achieved in circuits.

- The open-loop voltage gain A_{ol} is very high. Values to 200,000 are common.

- Slew rate is a measure of the op-amp's ability to change output voltages rapidly when input voltage changes in steps. A typical value of slew rate is 0.5 V/µs.

NEGATIVE FEEDBACK AND OP-AMPS

- Negative feedback takes a part of the output signal and feeds it back to the input out of phase with the input signal. This reduces the voltage gain of the amplifier.

- A noninverting amplifier has the input signal applied to the noninverting input. The input and output voltages are in phase.

- The voltage gain can be calculated by $A_V = (R_f/R_i) + 1$.

- A voltage-follower amplifier has a voltage gain of 1. It makes an excellent buffer amplifier with high input and low output impedances.

- An inverting amplifier has the input on the inverting input to the op-amp. The output signal is out of phase with the input signal.

- The voltage gain of an inverting amplifier is found by $A_V = -R_f/R_i$. The negative sign indicates an inversion.

- The input impedance of an inverting amplifier equals the value of R_i. $Z_{in} = R_i$.

- Virtual ground is the voltage between the two inputs. It is for all practical purposes zero volts.

TECHNICIAN TIPS

- The ability of an op-amp to reject noise is an important advantage. If an op-amp is supplied signals from a considerable distance away, a long pair of conductors is used. These conductors may pass strong magnetic fields for example, inducing noise voltages into both conductors equally. Since the signal is usually between one lead and ground, the op-amp's CMRR will reject, or not amplify, the noise voltages. The signal voltage will be amplified as desired. A CMRR of 80 dB is common and this represents a rejection ratio of 10,000. The signal voltage will be amplified 10,000 times more that the noise voltages.

- Input offset voltage errors sometime require correction to make sure the output voltage is zero when the input voltages are equal. Slight unbalances in the internal transistors can cause the output voltage be other than zero. Most op-amps have offset null terminals. Usually a 10-kΩ potentiometer is connected across these terminals with the wiper or center terminal connected to $-V_{CC}$.

CHAPTER 21 QUIZ

Student Name ____

1. The ideal amplifier has zero gain, infinite input impedance, and zero output impedance.
   a. true
   b. false

2. Slew rate is the rate that the output voltage of an op-amp can change in response to a step input.
   a. true
   b. false

3. Common-mode rejection ratio, CMRR, is a measure of an op-amp's ability to reject signals that appear the same on each input.
   a. true
   b. false

4. In an inverting amplifier, $Z_{in} = R_i$.
   a. true
   b. false

5. The open-loop voltage gain of an op-amp is usually small.
   a. true
   b. false

6. Which of the following terminals of an op-amp provides a 180° phase shift at the output?
   a. V_{CC}
   b. inverting
   c. noninverting
   d. offset null

7. A typical op-amp has ________ input impedance and ______ output impedance.
   a. high, high
   b. low, low
   c. low, high
   d. high, low

8. An op-amp uses ___________ feedback to control its ___________ gain.
   a. positive, voltage
   b. negative, impedance
   c. negative, voltage
   d. positive, current

9. See Figure 21-1(a). This circuit is known as
   a. a noninverting amplifier.
   b. an inverting amplifier.
   c. an open-loop amplifier.
   d. a voltage-follower amplifier.

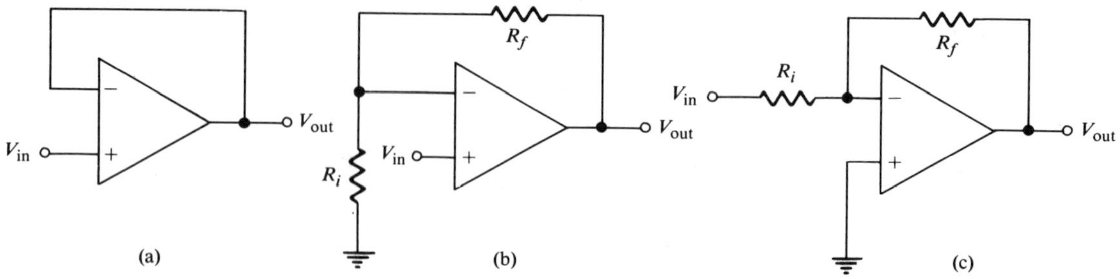

FIGURE 21-1

10. See Figure 21-1(b). This circuit is known as
   a. a noninverting amplifier.
   b. an inverting amplifier.
   c. an open-loop amplifier.
   d. a voltage-follower amplifier.

11. See Figure 21-1(c). This circuit is known as
   a. a noninverting amplifier.
   b. an inverting amplifier.
   c. an open-loop amplifier.
   d. a voltage-follower amplifier.

12. See Figure 21-1(b). If R_f = 470 kΩ and R_i = 5 kΩ, the voltage gain is
   a. 1
   b. 470
   c. 95
   d. 94

13. See Figure 21-1(c). If R_f = 150 kΩ and R_i = 10 kΩ, the voltage gain is
   a. 10
   b. 1
   c. 15
   d. 16

14. See Figure 21-1(a). This circuit is used as
   a. a high-gain amplifier.
   b. a buffer amplifier.
   c. an inverting amplifier.
   d. an oscillator.

15. An op-amp has a CMRR of 25,000. Expressed in dB, this would be
    a. 88 dB
    b. 44 dB
    c. 25,000 dB
    d. -44 dB

16. An op-amp has a slew rate of 0.25 V/μs. How long will it take the output voltage to go from -15 V to +15 V?
    a. 48 μs
    b. 120 μs
    c. 7.5 μs
    d. 3.75 μs

17. See Figure 21-1(c). R_f = 100 kΩ and A_V = 80. What is Z_{in}?
    a. 100 kΩ
    b. 80 kΩ
    c. 12.5 kΩ
    d. 1.25 kΩ

18. You wish to have an amplifier that will invert the signal, have a voltage gain of 25, and an input impedance of 10 kΩ. What type of amplifier should be used? What value should R_f have?
    a. noninverting, 250 kΩ
    b. inverting, 250 kΩ
    c. voltage-follower, 250 kΩ
    d. inverting, 240 kΩ

19. The output voltage of an inverting amplifier has the same value
    a. as V_{in}
    b. as V_{Ri}
    c. as V_{Rf}
    d. V_{CC}

20. A characteristic of a noninverting amplifier is
    a. a very high input impedance.
    b. a voltage gain of one.
    c. a phase inversion between input and output.
    d. a low input impedance.

REVIEW OF KEY POINTS IN CHAPTER 22

BASIC APPLICATIONS OF OP-AMPS

COMPARATORS

- Op-amps are often used to compare one signal voltage to another. In this use they are called comparators. A reference voltage is placed on one input and the signal on the other.
- If the reference voltage is zero, the circuit is a zero-level detector.
- A voltage level other than zero can be used. In this case a comparator is used as a nonzero-level detector.
- The open-loop gain is so large that the op-amp will saturate in either the + or - direction. $V_{sat} = V_{CC} - 2$ V. This is an approximate value.

SUMMING AMPLIFIERS

- Any number of separate signals may be input into an inverting amplifier with no interference between inputs. When an inverting amplifier is used this way, it is called a summing amplifier or adder.
- The output of a summing amplifier is the inverted sum of all the inputs. The only limitation to the number of inputs is the maximum output current of the op-amp.
- If the input resistances are all equal to R_f, then true addition will occur.
- Changing the values of R_i for any input will enable you to scale or multiply the sum by the individual voltage gains.
- An averaging amplifier can be made by setting the ratio R_f/R equal to the reciprocal of the number of inputs. This circuit will now take the average of all the inputs and place this value at the output.

INTEGRATORS AND DIFFERENTIATORS

- An inverting amplifier with a capacitor in place of the feedback resistor is called an **integrator.**
- This integrating circuit will produce a linear triangle wave output with a square wave input. Any other waveform will also be integrated.
- If the position of the capacitor and resistor are switched, the circuit is called a **differentiator.**
- A differentiating circuit will produce a square wave output from a triangle wave input and differentiate other waveforms.
- A sawtooth generator can be made with an integrator and a programmable unijunction transistor, PUT.

OP-AMP OSCILLATORS

- A Wien-bridge oscillator uses an op-amp and a lead-lag RC network to provide the necessary positive feedback.
- Wien-bridge oscillators provide an excellent sine wave output.
- Other types of oscillators, such as Hartley, Colpitts, Clapp, and crystal oscillators can also use op-amps.

ACTIVE FILTERS

- Op-amps are used extensively as filters. As such, they are called active filters.
- A simple active filter places an RC low- or high-pass filter before the input to an op-amp. In this case the cutoff frequency is found by $f_c = 1/2\pi RC$. This is a first-order filter that will produce a -20 dB/decade roll-off beginning at f_c.
- A Butterworth filter produces a very flat amplitude in the pass band.

- A second-order Butterworth high- or low-pass filter can be built using only one op-amp. A roll-off of -40 dB/decade is produced with this filter.

- A band-pass filter can be operated using two op-amps. One op-amp as a high-pass filter, and the other as a low-pass filter.

THREE-TERMINAL REGULATORS

- A three-terminal voltage regulator has an input, output, and a ground connection.

- A basic series regulator is made of an error-amplifier made of a noninverting op-amp circuit. If the load voltage changes, this voltage error is sensed by the op-amp, amplified, and a series-pass transistor is turned on or off a little to regulate the output voltage.

- Short-circuit and overload protection can be built into the regulator circuit.

- A shunt regulator uses a transistor to shunt part of the load current. This in turn keeps the output voltage at a nearly constant level.

TECHNICIAN TIPS

- An op-amp comparator used as a crossing detector is useful in many applications. By varying the reference voltage, the output pulse width can be varied. A pulse-width modulator, PWM, can be made from this circuit. These circuits are used in switching regulators. These regulators are efficient voltage regulators. Industrial control circuits also use op-amp comparators in many applications.

- An op-amp summing amplifier with potentiometers as input resistors can be used in an audio mixing circuit. The potentiometers provide variable gain for each input. A master gain control could use a potentiometer as R_f. Actual circuits would require buffer amplifiers between each input and the variable resistors to keep the input impedance of each input constant.

- Three-terminal regulators are a family of integrated circuit regulators that have the series-pass regulator, the op-amp error amplifier, and the over-current protection all in a single package. Once installed, these regulators are very durable; in an overload condition, they will shut down until the overload condition is gone. They are available in all popular voltage ratings in both positive and negative voltage outputs.

CHAPTER 22 QUIZ

Student Name ____________________

1. In an op-amp comparator, when the input voltage exceeds a specified reference voltage, the output changes state.
   a. true
   b. false

2. The terminals on a three-terminal regulator are input voltage, output voltage, and V_{CC}.
   a. true
   b. false

3. A series voltage regulator has the transistor in series with the load current.
   a. true
   b. false

4. A Wien-bridge oscillator provides an excellent sine wave output.
   a. true
   b. false

5. Butterworth filters are characterized by a very nonlinear response in the pass band.
   a. true
   b. false

6. See Figure 22-1. If V_1 = 6 V, find V_{OUT}?
   a. 1 V
   b. -1 V
   c. 13 V
   d. -13 V

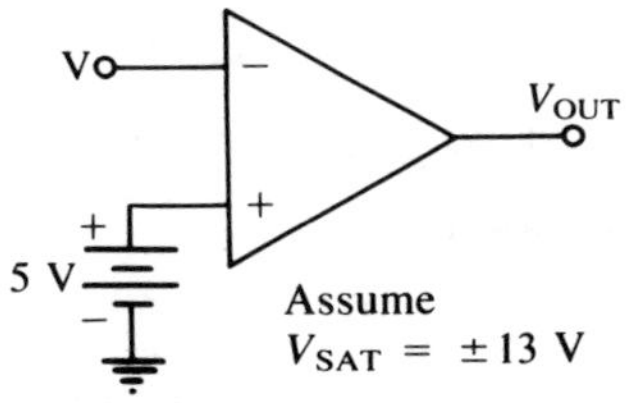

FIGURE 22-1

7. See Figure 22-1. If V_1 = -3 V, find V_{OUT}.
   a. 1 V
   b. -1 V
   c. 13 V
   d. -13 V

8. See Figure 22-1. If the voltage on the noninverting input were changed to -17 V and V_1 = -16.5 V, V_{OUT} would equal
   a. 1 V
   b. -1 V
   c. 13 V
   d. -13 V

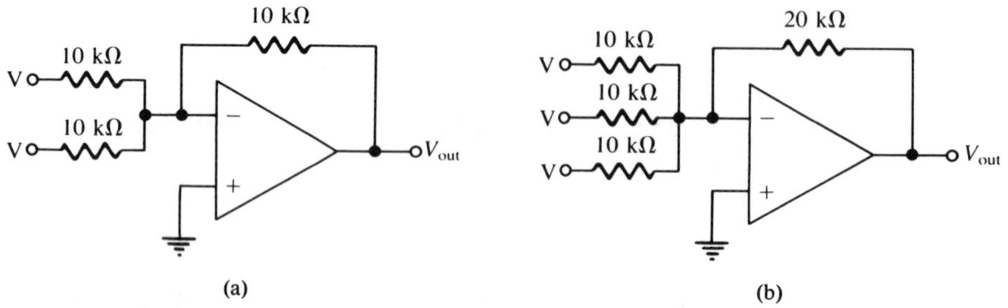

FIGURE 22-2

9. See Figure 22-2(a). This circuit is best known as
   a. a noninverting amplifier.
   b. an inverting amplifier.
   c. a summing amplifier.
   d. an integrator amplifier.

10. See Figure 22-2(a). If the two input voltages are -7.1 V and 12 V respectively, what is the output voltage?
   a. -4.9 V
   b. 4.9 V
   c. 19.1 V
   d. -19.1 V

11. See Figure 22-2(a). If the two inputs are -1.7 V and -2.6 V, what is the output voltage?
   a. 0.9 V
   b. -0.9 V
   c. -4.3 V
   d. 4.3 V

12. See Figure 22-2(b). If the three inputs are 1.7 V, -0.6 V, and 2.4 V respectively, what is the output voltage?
   a. 7 V
   b. -7 V
   c. -1.4 V
   d. 1.4 V

13. See Figure 22-2(b). If the three inputs are -1.4 V, -0.9 V, and 0.7 V, respectively, what is the output voltage?
a. -1.6 V
b. 1.6 V
c. 3.2 V
d. -3.2 V

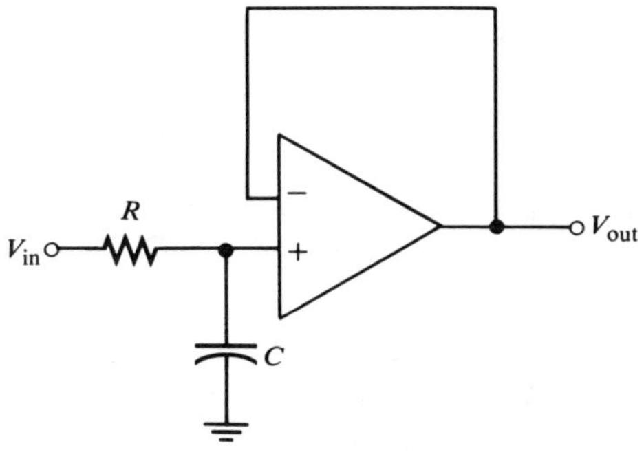

FIGURE 22-3

14. See Figure 22-3. This circuit is known as a ________________, and it has a rolloff of ______________.
a. high-pass filter, -20 dB/decade
b. low-pass filter, -20 dB/decade
c. band-pass filter, -20 dB/decade
d. low-pass filter, -40 dB/decade

15. See Figure 22-3. If R = 22 kΩ and C = 0.05 µF, find f_{co}.
a. 1.45 kHz
b. 23 Hz
c. 145 Hz
d. 2.3 kHz

16. See Figure 22-3. If V_{in} = 17 V_{p-p}, what is the output voltage at f_{co}?
a. 12 V_{dc}
b. 24 V_{p-p}
c. 12 V_{p-p}
d. 17 V_{RMS}

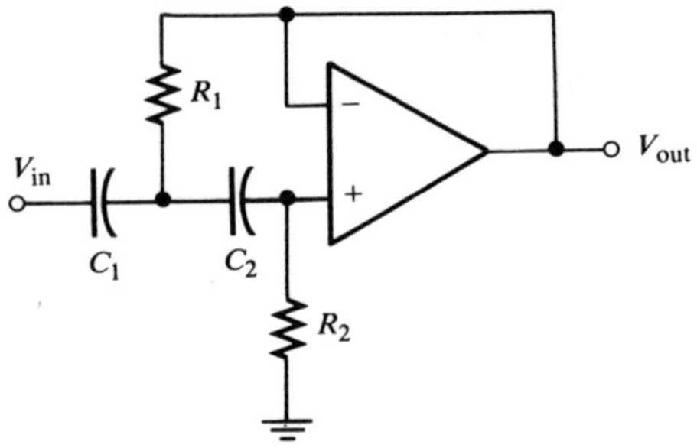

FIGURE 22-4

17. See Figure 22-4. This circuit is known as ________________, and it has a rolloff of ________________.
    a. a Butterworth high-pass filter, -40 dB/decade
    b. a Butterworth low-pass filter, -40 dB/decade
    c. a Butterworth high-pass filter, -20 dB/decade
    d. a Butterworth low-pass filter, -20 dB/decade

18. See Figure 22-4. This circuit could also be called a
    a. single-pole, active high-pass filter.
    b. two-pole, active high-pass filter.
    c. two-pole, active low-pass filter.
    d. single-pole, active low-pass filter.

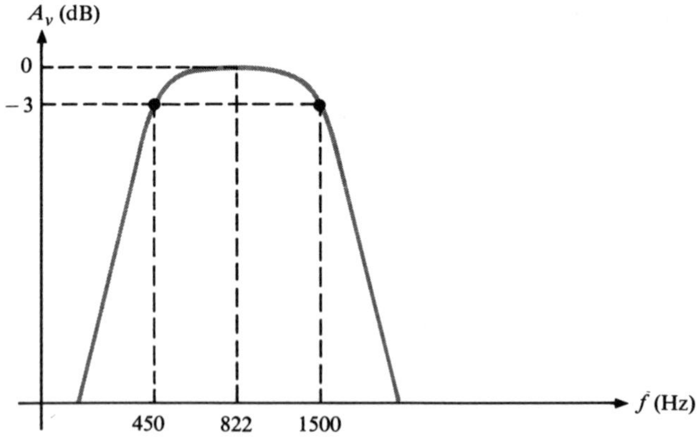

FIGURE 22-5

19. See Figure 22-5. This curve represents the output from a
    a. low-pass filter.
    b. high-pass filter.
    c. band-pass filter.
    d. band-reject filter.

20. See Figure 22-5. If V_{OUT} at 822 Hz equals 27.4 V, what is the output at 1.5 kHz?
    a. 27.4 V
    b. 19.37 V
    c. 13.7 V
    d. 6.85 V

APPENDIX

ANSWERS TO CHAPTER QUIZZES

	Chapter 1	Chapter 2	Chapter 3	Chapter 4	Chapter 5	Chapter 6
1.	A	B	B	B	A	A
2.	A	A	A	A	B	B
3.	A	B	B	B	A	A
4.	A	A	A	A	B	B
5.	A	B	A	B	A	A
6.	E	C	B	B	A	E
7.	C	B	D	C	B	C
8.	B	D	D	D	D	A
9.	E	D	B	A	B	B
10.	C	D	A	C	D	B
11.	E	A	C	A	C	C
12.	B	D	C	D	C	D
13.	C	B	C	A	D	A
14.	B	D	A	B	C	B
15.	D	A	B	C	B	B
16.	D	D	C	B	A	D
17.	B	B	D	A	C	A
18.	B	C	C	B	D	A
19.	C	B	C	B	B	B
20.	B	C	B	B	C	A

	Chapter 7	Chapter 8	Chapter 9	Chapter 10	Chapter 11	Chapter 12
1.	B	B	A	A	A	A
2.	A	A	B	B	B	B
3.	A	B	A	B	B	B
4.	A	A	B	A	A	A
5.	A	B	A	A	B	A
6.	A	D	B	D	A	C
7.	C	B	D	A	D	B
8.	B	C	D	D	C	A
9.	D	C	C	B	D	D
10.	C	B	D	C	C	C
11.	A	A	A	A	A	D
12.	B	D	C	C	C	B
13.	A	D	B	C	A	B
14.	D	B	A	D	D	A
15.	D	A	C	C	B	C
16.	C	D	B	D	C	D
17.	C	C	C	B	A	C
18.	B	B	A	B	C	B
19.	C	A	D	A	B	A
20.	A	C	C	C	A	B

Chapter 13	Chapter 14	Chapter 15	Chapter 16	Chapter 17	Chapter 18
1. B	1. B	1. A	1. B	1. A	1. B
2. A	2. A	2. B	2. A	2. A	2. A
3. A	3. A	3. A	3. A	3. B	3. A
4. A	4. A	4. B	4. B	4. B	4. B
5. B	5. B	5. A	5. B	5. A	5. A
6. A	6. B	6. C	6. A	6. C	6. C
7. C	7. C	7. D	7. C	7. A	7. B
8. D	8. D	8. A	8. D	8. D	8. D
9. B	9. A	9. B	9. B	9. B	9. B
10. C	10. D	10. D	10. C	10. C	10. A
11. B	11. A	11. B	11. A	11 D	11. C
12. C	12. D	12. C	12. D	12. B	12. B
13. A	13. B	13. A	13. B	13. A	13. C
14. C	14. B	14. B	14. B	14. D	14. A
15. A	15. C	15. D	15. B	15. D	15. D
16. C	16. D	16. C	16. C	16. A	16. A
17. A	17. B	17. B	17. A	17. C	17. D
18. B	18. A	18. C	18. B	18. D	18. B
19. D	19. B	19. A	19. D	19. A	19. D
20. C	20. C	20. B	20. D	20. B	20. D

Chapter 19	Chapter 20	Chapter 21	Chapter 22
1. B	1. A	1. B	1. A
2. A	2. B	2. A	2. B
3. A	3. B	3. A	3. A
4. B	4. A	4. A	4. A
5. A	5. A	5. B	5. B
6. A	6. C	6. B	6. D
7. B	7. C	7. D	7. C
8. C	8. A	8. C	8. D
9. D	9. D	9. D	9. C
10. B	10. B	10. A	10. A
11. D	11. B	11. B	11. D
12. C	12. A	12. C	12. B
13. A	13. C	13. C	13. C
14. C	14. B	14. B	14. B
15. A	15. C	15. A	15. C
16. B	16. B	16. B	16. C
17. C	17. C	17. D	17. A
18. D	18. A	18. B	18. B
19. D	19. C	19. C	19. C
20. C	20. B	20. A	20. B